A Practical Course of English Pronunciation
A perceptual approach

A C Gimson
Professor of Phonetics
University College London

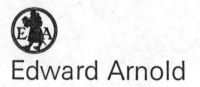

Edward Arnold

First published 1975
by Edward Arnold (Publishers) Ltd,
25 Hill Street, London W1X 8LL

Cloth edition ISBN: 0 7131 5795 X
Paper edition ISBN: 0 7131 5796 8

Printed in Great Britain by
William Clowes & Sons, Limited
London, Beccles and Colchester

A Practical Course
of English Pronunciation

Foreword

I have been urged for some time since the first appearance of my *Introduction to the Pronunciation of English* in 1962 to prepare a companion handbook which would be specifically designed for the foreign learner. The present, short *Practical Course* is therefore concerned less with a theoretical descriptive statement of the pronunciation of English than with those considerations which are immediately relevant to the foreign learner's difficulties.

The approach is perceptual in that the course relies heavily on training the learner's skills in auditory discrimination as a prerequisite to his own performance. The recordings (available on tape or cassette) form a necessary part of the course, and permit its use by individual learners who possess playback facilities as well as by those who study under the direction of a teacher and with the help of a language laboratory. The two hours of recording containing some 330 drills can be studied by the learner in such units as correspond to his needs and to the time which he has available.

Thirty years' experience of teaching pronunciation to foreign learners of English have made it clear that it requires constant and assiduous practice to instil new phonetic skills, especially in the adult whose incorrectly-acquired habits have so often to be eliminated. This *Course* follows the well-tried teaching practices which have become established in the Department of Phonetics and Linguistics at University College London. I gratefully acknowledge the advice freely given by my colleagues and the enlightenment provided constantly and often unwittingly by my students.

September 1974
University College London   G

Contents

Section 4   Accentuation and rhythm   33

Section 1
Introduction

1.1   Purpose of the course

The operation of language consists of the formulation of the message which we wish to express, the choice of the appropriate words and their organization according to the grammatical rules of the language in question, the transmission of the message by speech or writing, the reception (auditory or visual) of the message, and its interpretation by the listener or reader. If the essence of language is its grammar, communication by language clearly relies crucially on the effectiveness of the transmission phase, i.e. for our purposes, the easy intelligibility of the pronunciation.

The pronunciation of a second language poses problems of a different kind from those which we face when we learn our first language. In the latter case, we are exposed to the sound of the language throughout every day; yet, nevertheless, it is five to six years before our performance begins to approximate to adult standards of competence. During this time, the sound system of our own language assumes an increasing dominance, so that eventually we tend to hear all speech sounds in terms of our own system. When we embark upon the acquisition of the pronunciation of a second language, the first requirement is to overcome the pronunciation prejudices which have become instilled in us—and the older we are when we begin, the more important and difficult is the task. Before we try to produce sounds which are new to us, it is therefore essential that we should perceive the differences between the sounds in the new language, and between the new sounds and those of our own language with which we have become so familiar. This is what the present course sets out to do: drills of listening and discrimination, and only then attempts at performance.

Such a perceptual approach requires from the learner only the minimum of theoretical knowledge. In any case, articulatory instructions are on the whole useful only for the acquisition of consonant sounds; for the other elements, auditory control is crucial. For this reason, the theoretical commentary in this course is restricted to essentials. For more detailed theoretical information, such as might be needed by a teacher or a more advanced student, the user is referred throughout the course to my *Introduction to the Pronunciation of English* (second edition, London, Edward Arnold, 1970); e.g. a student requiring more information on the aspiration of plosives is referred to the relevant section by means of the abbreviation '*IPE* 8.03'.

1.2   Pronunciation systems (*IPE* Ch. 5)

The pronunciation system of a language operates with a finite number of significant elements, which it is the learner's first task to distinguish in listening and speaking. For English, these may conveniently be divided into two categories: the segmental elements (the vowel and consonant sounds) and the prosodic elements (accentuation and intonation). It is important to note, however, especially with regard to the sounds, that the distinctive elements (the 'phonemes') will be realized in different ways according to the situation in which they occur. Thus, the realization of the phoneme /eɪ/ in *day* is longer than that in *date*; the two occurrences of /l/ in *little* are noticeably different. In this course, we are concerned mainly with the phonemes (the symbols for which are enclosed in / /), but, when we wish to distinguish varieties within the phoneme, we enclose the symbols in [ ], e.g. the two *l* sounds in *little* will be shown as [l] and [ɫ]. Similarly, in intonation, there are variations of realization of the essential elements, e.g. a falling tone on *no* will consist of a continuous glide, but the same tone on *better* may well be realized in two steps. In the case of intonation, however, it is necessary to distinguish between variants which depend on the phonetic and pitch context and those which signal a different mood of the speaker.

1.3   Standards of performance

Undoubtedly the minimum standard of performance which any ordinary learner should aim at is one which is easily understood by the native speaker of English. Native speaker response is the crucial consideration. It is not sufficient for the learner to be easily intelligible when speaking English to a listener of his own nationality. In such a situation he may achieve high intelligibility by using the sound system of his own language, while the English listener might not recognize the language spoken as English at all. If, however, the learner masters the essential elements presented in this course, together with the main contextual variants, he should give no difficulty to the English listener. Whether or not he sounds precisely like an Englishman will depend on the level of his achievement (to achieve such a goal there has also to be high competence in the use of grammatical structures and the choice of semantically and culturally appropriate vocabulary), but there will be no serious phonetic obstacle to easy communication.

For the teacher, however, easy intelligibility is not enough. He has the added responsibility of serving as a model for his pupils, who, if they are young, will imitate equally well a correct or a faulty pronunciation. His aim therefore must be perfection in respect of all aspects of pronunciation.

Of course, all the elements of the sound system may be regarded as equally important for good communication, but in English as in any other language there is great redundancy in the information conveyed by speech: the native listener may make use of only half of all the speech signals which he receives. He is predisposed, for instance, by the linguistic context and the general situation to expect to hear and understand certain utterances. This does not mean, however, that the foreign learner may disregard half of the pronunciation system of English. Gross errors of pronunciation seriously distract attention and interfere with the communication process, however adequate the remainder of the utterance may be. Nothing, for instance, is more confusing to the English listener than mistakes of accentuation (rhythm and the associated obscuration of certain syllables). If, therefore, priority is to be given to any of the following sections, it is to the section on accentuation and rhythm that particular attention should be paid.

Command of the transmission phase of a language, however, is not only concerned with performance. The learner must also be able to understand English as spoken normally by native speakers. In this course, all examples are recorded at a natural speed such as might be used in ordinary conversation. Again, it is emphasized that the learner should devote as much time to listening as to performance.

1.4   The type of English

This course is concerned with British English. But within Britain there are a great number of different varieties of pronunciation. The type here described and used in the recordings is that which has traditionally been called 'received pronunciation' (RP), which is basically the educated speech form of the south-eastern region of Britain (*IPE* 6.3–6.32). It is the form generally used by news-readers of the BBC and has the advantage (shared by few other forms of British English) of being readily intelligible and acceptable within the English-speaking world. The fact that descriptions and recordings of British English pronunciation used for teaching English as a foreign language invariably refer to this form is also a powerful reason for its choice.

It has to be remembered, however, that the pronunciation of a language changes perceptibly in time. Older, conservative forms are avoided in this course, as are sporadic innovations used by 'advanced' speakers, for these latter are as likely to be ephemeral as they are to be markers of incipient change. Distinct changes are rarely discernible except over the span of a century. The pronunciation here used is known as 'general' RP, i.e. the form which is typical of the middle generations in the last half of the twentieth century (*IPE* 6.32(5)).

1.5   How to use the course

Learners with different linguistic backgrounds will obviously have different pronunciation difficulties in approaching English. It is for each teacher to decide which elements must be concentrated upon and with what degree of emphasis. For instance, learners with relatively simple vowel systems in their own language (e.g. Spanish or Italian) will need to devote considerable time to the English complex vowel system; learners with a strong accentual system in their language (e.g. in German or Russian) will need to pay less attention to accentuation than those with a less dynamic system (e.g. in French or some Indian languages); learners who speak tone languages (e.g. many Oriental and African languages and, to some extent, Norwegian and Swedish) will have especial problems with intonation; on the other hand, the majority of learners are likely to have difficulty with the complex consonant clusters which occur in English.

It is important that users of this course should quickly familiarize themselves with the system of phonetic transcription employed (see p. 7). It is only by means of such a transcription that English pronunciation can be unambiguously indicated.

The recordings accompanying the course are an integral part of it. The drills are identified in the text, the recording and the Appendix by a letter and a number, e.g. **V10** indicates the tenth drill of the Vowel section. Various instructions are given in the text, and these should be interpreted as follows:

(1) *Listen*

The learner should listen to the examples more than once, so that a firm auditory impression is established.

(2) *Identify*

In such drills, the user should make discriminatory decisions either as between English sounds or as between English and non-English sounds. He may then refer to the Appendix for the correct answers.

(3) *Transcribe*

In a few cases, the user is advised to transcribe phonetically what he hears (English or nonsense) or words given in the text. Again, the correct transcription will be found in the Appendix.

(4) *Listen and repeat*

Most drills take this form. There are pauses between items to allow the learner to imitate what he hears. If he has facilities for recording his responses, he should compare his performance with the model. These drills should be played as many times as is necessary. Additional examples for performance practice are to be found in *IPE*.

(5) *Notes*

Most sections are prefaced by brief notes on the elements to be drilled. These notes are intended to provide basic information essential for the learner. For more detail, reference is made to the relevant sections of *IPE*.

Finally, it is essential that a learner should not proceed from one drill to another in the same section until complete adequacy in discrimination and performance is achieved.

Phonetic symbols

Sounds (ː = length)

iː	bean	ɪ	pit	eɪ	bay
ɑː	barn	e	pet	aɪ	buy
ɔː	born	æ	pat	ɔɪ	boy
uː	boon	ʌ	putt	əʊ	no
ɜː	burn	ɒ	pot	aʊ	now
		ʊ	put	ɪə	peer
		ə	another	ɛə	pair
				ʊə	poor

p	pin	f	fine	l	let
b	bin	v	vine	ɫ	fill
t	tin	θ	think	l̩	play
d	din	ð	this	r	red
k	come	s	seal	ɹ̩	pray
g	gum	z	zeal	m	my
tʃ	chain	ʃ	sheep	n	no
dʒ	Jane	ʒ	measure	ŋ	sing
		h	how	j	yes
				w	wet

Accentuation

ˋ	or	'	primary accent
•	or	ˌ	secondary accent
○		unaccented syllable with strong vowel
•		unaccented syllable with weak vowel or syllabic consonant

Intonation: Nuclear Tones

ˎ	low-fall	ˋ	high-fall	ˏ	low-rise
ˊ	high-rise	˅	fall-rise	˄	rise-fall

Section 2
Vowels

2.1   Vowel phonemes (*IPE* Ch. 7)

There are 20 distinctive items (phonemes) in the RP vowel system.
These may be classified as follows:

(a) 5 *long:*   bean boon barn born burn
   /   iː   uː   ɑː   ɔː   ɜː   /
(b) 7 *short:*   pit pet pat putt pot put
   /   ɪ   e   æ   ʌ   ɒ   ʊ   /
      and   /ə/ (only in unaccented syllables, e.g. '*another*')
(c) 8 *diphthongs:*
   (1) gliding to [ɪ]:   bay buy boy
      /   eɪ   aɪ   ɔɪ   /
   (2) gliding to [ʊ]:   no now
      /   əʊ   ɑʊ   /
   (3) gliding to [ə]:   peer pair poor
      /   ɪə   ɛə   ʊə   /

2.2   Long vowels

   bean boon barn born burn
/   iː   uː   ɑː   ɔː   ɜː   /

Notes:
(a) /iː, uː/ resemble for practical purposes similar vowels in
other languages (*IPE* 7.09, 7.18).
(b) /ɑː/ is a back open vowel (*IPE* 7.14).
(c) /ɜː/ is a central vowel said with neutral lips (*IPE* 7.19).
(d) /ɔː/ is a mid back vowel with medium lip-rounding (*IPE*
7.16).
(e) for /ɜː, ɑː, ɔː/ any *r* in the spelling is not pronounced when
final or before a consonant.

V1   *Listen*
/iː, uː, ɑː, ɔː, ɜː; ɑː, ɜː, ɔː, iː, uː/

V2   *Identify* the vowels; write the appropriate symbol, and check in Appendix p. 73.

V3   *Identify* the vowels; some are not English; write the symbols for the English vowels, and mark the non-English sounds with **X**; check in Appendix p. 73.

V4   *Listen and repeat*
/ɔː, uː, ɜː, iː, ɑː, ɜː, ɔː, uː, ɜː, ɑː, ɔː, ɜː, ɑː, ɔː, ɜː/

V5   *Listen and repeat*
see   car   law   shoe   fur
seen   card   lord   food   bird

2.3   Reduced long vowels (*IPE* 7.04)

Note: Long vowels have their length considerably reduced when they occur in a syllable closed by /p, t, k, tʃ, f, θ, s, ʃ/, e.g. in *soup, seat, leak, porch, half, earth, loose, leash.* This shortening of the vowel is highly significant in distinguishing a word such as *seat* from *seed.*

V6   *Listen*
seed   seat   lose   loose   halve   half   four   fork   surge   search

V7   *Identify* in the following words those vowels which are pronounced too long; check in Appendix p. 73.
search   lark   feet   fought   shoot   heart   hoop   hurt   north   loose   teach   sauce   pass

V8   *Listen and repeat*
search   lark   feet   fought   shoot
heart   hoop   hurt   north   loose
teach   sauce   pass   purse   staff

V9   *Listen and repeat* (long vowels in their full and reduced forms)
feed   hurt   half   loose   saw   heard   feet
halve   peas   purse   sauce   purrs   peace   lose

2.4 Short vowels

pit pet pat putt pot put another
/ ɪ   e   æ   ʌ   ɒ   ʊ   ə-ʌ-ə /

Notes:

(a) /ɪ, e, æ/ are front vowels (*IPE* 7.10, 7.11, 7.12); /ɪ/ is centralized and lowered compared with /iː/; /æ/, between the *e* and
a vowels of many languages, is often considerably lengthened
before /b, d, g, dʒ, m, n/, e.g. in *bad, bag*.

(b) /ʌ/ is a central to front vowel with neutral lips (*IPE* 7.13).

(c) /ɒ/ is a back open vowel with slight open lip-rounding
(*IPE* 7.15).

(d) /ʊ/ is centralized and lowered compared with /uː/; weak lip-
rounding (*IPE* 7.17).

(e) /ə/ is a central vowel occurring only in unaccented syllables;
neutral lips (*IPE* 7.20).

V10 *Listen*
/ɪ, e, æ, ʌ, ɒ, ʊ, ə; ɒ, ʊ, ɪ, e, æ, ʌ, ə/

V11 *Identify* the vowels; write the appropriate symbol, and check
in the Appendix p. 73.

V12 *Identify* the vowels; some are not English; write the symbols
for the English vowels, and mark the non-English sounds
with **X**; check in Appendix p. 73.

V13 *Listen and repeat*
/ e   ɒ   ʊ   ɪ   ə   æ   ʌ
    ʊ   e   æ   ə   ɪ   ɒ   ʊ /

2.5 Comparison: short vowels

In the following drills, identify and then repeat the members of
pairs.

V14 *Identify*
/ɪ–e/ (Check in Appendix p. 73)

V15 *Listen and repeat*
bit bet sit set tin ten

V16 *Identify*
/e–æ/ (Check in Appendix p. 73)

V17 *Listen and repeat*
men man bed bad mess mass

V18 *Identify*
/æ–ʌ/ (Check in Appendix p. 73)

V19 *Listen and repeat*
cat cut lamp lump match much

V20 *Identify*
/ʌ–ɒ/ (Check in Appendix p. 73)

V21 *Listen and repeat*
cut cot wonder wander fund fond

V22 *Identify*
/ɪ–ə/ (Check in Appendix p. 73)

V23 *Listen and repeat*
offices   officers except accept
chattered chatted sitter city

V24 *Listen and repeat* (recapitulation: short vowels)
bet   good cat bit   much   waiter
city   man   dog another men   weighty
colour bad   son accept   collar gone

2.6   Comparison: long and short vowels

V25 *Listen*
/ iːd iːt ɪt; uːd uːt ʊt;
aːd aːt ʌt; ɔːd ɔːt ɒt;
ɔːd ɔːt ʊt; ɜːd ɜːt ət/

V26 *Identify* the vowels before /t/ and /d/; check in Appendix p. 73.

V27 *Listen and repeat*
Note: Remember that reduced long vowels become so short that they may be of about the same length as short vowels, e.g. *feet* and *fit* are distinguished for practical purposes only by quality.

feed	feet	fit
league	leak	lick
food	boot	foot
card	cart	cut
cord	caught	cot
sword	sort	soot
purrs	purse	purpose

V28   *Identify* the vowels; some are incorrect; write the symbols for the correct vowels, and mark the incorrect vowels with X; check in Appendix p. 73.

    (1) feet   (2) bed   (3) back   (4) gone   (5) taught
    (6) cut   (7) fit   (8) shirt   (9) come   (10) seat
    (11) man (12) good (13) cart (14) bird (15) hot
    (16) hard (17) boot (18) hit

V29   *Listen and repeat* (recapitulation: all vowels)

tea	head	big	bad	bus	dog	hurt	much
bid	teeth	live	want	bat	heard	mother	ham
ate	sick	heart	saw	doctor	women	tooth	

2.7   Diphthongs

Notes:
    (a) The main prominence is always on the first element of the diphthong, the second element being only lightly sounded.
    (b) Diphthongs undergo the same reduction of length before / p, t, k, tʃ, f, θ, s, ʃ/ as the long vowels.

2.8   Glides to [ɪ] (*IPE* 7.22, 7.23, 7.24)

  bay buy boy
/ eɪ   aɪ   ɔɪ /

V30   *Listen*
    /eɪ, aɪ, ɔɪ, aɪ, ɔɪ, eɪ, aɪ, eɪ, ɔɪ/

V31   *Identify* the diphthongs; write the appropriate symbol, and check in Appendix p. 74.

V32   *Identify* the diphthongs; some are incorrect, write the symbols for the correct diphthongs, and mark the incorrect ones with X; check in Appendix p. 74.

V33 *Listen and repeat*
pain boy lie made noise
wide shade fine avoid paid

V34 *Listen* (fully long: reduced)
side sight played plate noise voice

V35 *Identify* the diphthongs which are too long; check in Appendix p. 74.
fight wait choice place
light face joint like

V36 *Listen and repeat*
name mine joy day wide shape
like point taste voice ice join

V37 *Listen and repeat* (comparison /eɪ/—/e/)
sale sell waist west saint sent
pain pen late let

2.9 **Glides to [ʊ]** (*IPE* 7.25, 7.26)
no now
/əʊ aʊ /

V38 *Listen*
/əʊ, aʊ, aʊ, əʊ, aʊ, əʊ/

V39 *Identify* the diphthongs; write the appropriate symbol and check in Appendix p. 74.

V40 *Identify* the diphthongs; some are incorrect; write the symbols for the correct diphthongs, and mark the incorrect ones with **X**; check in Appendix p. 74.

V41 *Listen and repeat*
Note: /əʊ/ = /ɜː/ + /ʊ/
home cow so town how
low loud load sound goes

V42 *Listen* (fully long: reduced)
code coat found fount
road wrote house (*vb.*) house (*n.*)

V43   *Identify* the diphthongs which are too long; check in Appendix p. 74.

oak   shout   won't   couch
mouth   post   about   both

V44   *Listen and repeat*

go   town   soap   how
post   house   known   pound

V45   *Listen and repeat* (comparison /əʊ/—/ɜː/)

own   earn   coat   curt   foam   firm

V46   *Listen and repeat* (comparison /əʊ/—/ɔː/)

so   saw   load   lord   boat   bought

V47   *Listen and repeat* (comparison /əʊ/—/ɜː/—/ɔː/)

bone   burn   born   woke   work   walk

2.10   Sequences /aɪ, aʊ/ + /ə/ (*IPE* 7.27)

Note: Increasingly, the sequences /aɪə, aʊə/ have their second element weakened or eliminated. Thus, *tyre* /taɪə/ may be pronounced /taːə/ or /taː/; *tower* may be pronounced /taʊə/ or /taː/ (identical with *tar*). It is not incorrect to pronounce the full forms /aɪə, aʊə/, but in order to conform to current usage the learner is recommended to use /aːə, aːə/. (Note, however, the more fronted quality of the first element of /aːə/ as compared with that of /aːə/.)

V48   *Listen*

/taɪə, taːə, taː; taʊə, taːə, taː; taːə, taːə/

V49   *Listen and repeat*

tyre   tower   tar   fire   far
shire   shower   diary   dowry

2.11   Glides to [ə] (*IPE* 7.28)

peer   pair   poor
/ ɪə   ɛə   ʊə /

Notes:
   (a) /ɪə/ should begin with the centralized /ɪ/, not /iː/, and kept distinct from /ɛə/.

(b) /ʊə/ (a rare diphthong which increasingly is replaced by /ɔː/) should begin with /ʊ/, not /uː/.

V50 *Listen*
/ɪə, ɛə, ʊə, ɛə, ɪə, ʊə, ɛə, ɪə/

V51 *Identify* the diphthongs; write the appropriate symbol and check in Appendix p. 74.

V52 *Identify* the diphthongs; some are incorrect; write the symbols for the correct diphthongs, and mark the incorrect ones with **X**; check in Appendix p. 74.

V53 *Listen and repeat* (comparison /ɪə/—/ɛə/)
beer   bare   mere   mayor
fear   fair   dear   dare

V54 *Listen and repeat* (fully long: reduced)
fears   fierce   care   scarce   peers   pierce

V55 *Listen and repeat*
near   poor   pear   fierce   vary   hero
scarce   jury   pierce   there   theory   Europe
pure   idea   mayor   beer

2.12 Recapitulation: vowels and diphthongs

V56 *Identify* the vowels and diphthongs in the following nonsense words; write the vowel or diphthong symbol, and check in Appendix p. 74.

V57 *Identify* the vowels and diphthongs in the following nonsense words; write the appropriate symbols; some are incorrect—mark these with **X**; check in Appendix p. 74.

V58 *Listen* to the following words and *transcribe* them phonetically; check in Appendix p. 74.
disorganize   speedometer   repulsive   smallpox
soliloquy   locomotive   Essex   coalesce
paradox   countrymen   benefactor   work-basket

Listen again to the words in V58 and *Repeat*, imitating the rhythmic structure of the words.

V59 *Listen and repeat*

gas	saint	feed	hope	pin
another	house (*n.*)	cupboard	afternoon	winter
ghost	white	pocket	talking	Wednesday
boyhood	concert	birthday	football	homely
early	during	goodness	landlady	hollow
murder	power-station	department	bookshop	colour

Section 3
Consonants

3.1 Consonant phonemes (*IPE* Ch. 8)

There are 24 distinctive items (phonemes) in the RP consonant system, to which, for practical teaching purposes, /tr, dr/ may be added. These may be classified as follows:

(a) 6 *plosives:* pin bin   tin din   come gum
  / p   b   t   d   k   g /
(b) 4 *affricates:*   chain Jane train drain
  / tʃ   dʒ   tr   dr /
(c) 9 *fricatives:* fine vine think this seal
  / f   v   θ   ð   s
  zeal sheep measure how
  z   ʃ   ʒ   h /
(d) 3 *nasals:* sum sun sung
  / m   n   ŋ /
(e) 1 *lateral* and 1 *frictionless continuant:* light right
  / l   r /
(f) 2 *semi-vowels:* wet yet
  / w   j /

3.2 Plosives (*IPE* 8.02–8.08)

pin bin   tin din   come gum
/ p   b   t   d   k   g /

Notes: The main features which distinguish the English plosives are:
(a) place of articulation
(b) presence or absence of aspiration
(c) presence or absence of voicing
(d) length of preceding sounds.

3.3   Plosives: place of articulation (*IPE* 8.03(1))

Notes:
(a) The places are: bilabial /p, b/
                                  alveolar /t, d/
                                  velar /k, g/.
(b) /t, d/ are generally made with the tongue contact just behind the teeth, *not*, as in most languages, on the teeth (*IPE* 8.07(2)).
(c) Final plosives often have no audible explosion (*IPE* 8.05(1)).

C1   *Listen*
         pin tin kin   sip sit sick

C2   *Identify* the plosive in each word—/p, t, k, b, d/ or /g/; some have an incorrect place of articulation; mark these with **X**; check in Appendix p. 74.

C3   *Listen and repeat*
         gun   eight pipe tin   big
         take sob   kick ape   did

3.4   Plosives: aspiration (*IPE* 8.03 (2, 3))

Notes:
(a) In accented initial positions, the main feature distinguishing /p, t, k/ from /b, d, g/ is the aspiration (puff of air) associated with the former.
(b) Initially in unaccented syllables, /p, t, k/ are only weakly aspirated.
(c) After /s/, even in the case of an accented syllable, /p, t, k/ are unaspirated.

C4   *Listen*
         pin bin   town down   came game

C5   *Identify* the initial plosives in the following words; write the appropriate symbol; some cases of /p, t, k/ are unaspirated; mark these with **X**; check in Appendix p. 75.

C6   *Listen and repeat*
         card   town pie game   tie
         down   came die guard buy

C7 *Listen and repeat* (weaker aspiration of /p, t, k/ in unaccented syllables)
supper   letter   maker   after   sleeping
income   matter   lucky   happy

C8 *Listen* (absence of aspiration of /p, t, k/ after /s/)
pin   spin   bin   tore   store   door   come   scum
gum

C9 *Identify* the plosives in the following words; some are incorrectly aspirated after /s/; mark these with **X**; check in Appendix p. 75.

C10 *Listen and repeat*
Note: Take care not to insert a vowel before /s/.
skin   steam   spy   stay   scheme   spit

3.5 Plosives: voicing[1] in medial positions (*IPE* 8.03(4))

Note: Voicing is used as a distinguishing feature between /p, t, k/ and /b, d, g/ in medial unaccented positions, aspiration on /p, t, k/ being weak.

C11 *Listen and repeat*
rapid   rabid   latter   ladder   bicker   bigger

3.6 Plosives: length of preceding sounds (*IPE* 8.03(5))—see also sections 2.3, 2.7 of this course.

Notes:
(a) Long vowels and diphthongs (and in some cases /æ/) are shorter before /p, t, k/ than before /b, d, g/, thus providing an important cue to the plosive.
(b) /l/ is also shorter before /p, t, k/ than before /b, d, g/
/n/ is also shorter before /t/ than before /d/
/m/ is also shorter before /p/ than before /b/.

---

[1] 'Voicing' is the vibration of the vocal folds which distinguishes /z/ from /s/ (*IPE* 2.22).

C12   *Listen and repeat*
tripe   tribe   seat   seed   leak   league
water   warder   paper   labour   pulp   bulb
meant   mend   kilt   killed

3.7   Plosive clusters (*IPE* 8.05(2))

Note: When a plosive is followed by another plosive or an affricate (/tʃ, dʒ, tr, dr/), within a word or at word boundaries, there is no intervening sound (either aspiration [ʰ] or a vowel).

C13   *Listen*
captain   football   locked   actor
good boy   ripe cheese   white chalk

C14   *Identify* in the following items those cases where there is an intrusive [ʰ] or vowel between the plosive and the following plosive or affricate; check in Appendix p. 75.
licked   that pen   wiped   top dog
night time   goodbye   blackboard   sector

C15   *Listen and repeat*
sickbay   that chair   good game   topcoat
doctor   begged   locked   sobbed   helped

3.8   Plosive + /m/ or /n/ (*IPE* 8.05(4))

Note: When /p, b/ are followed by /m/ or, more commonly, /t, d/ by /n/, the plosive is released through the nose, without an intervening [ʰ] or vowel.

C16   *Listen*
topmost   submerge   cotton
sudden   chutney   goodness

C17   *Listen* ('a' here = any vowel)
(1) apma   (2) apʰma   (3) abma   (4) ab°ma   (5) atna
(6) atʰna   (7) atn   (8) atʰn   (9)adn   (10 ad°n

C18   *Identify* those items which have an intrusive [ʰ] or vowel between the plosive and the nasal; check in Appendix p. 75.
shipmate   submit   mutton   garden
written   red nose   madness

C19 *Listen and repeat*
eaten   burden   submarine   button
hidden   didn't   not nearly   suddenly

C20 *Listen and repeat*
Note: /ə/ is kept in the endings /-ntən, -ndən/.
London   wanton   abandon   lantern

3.9 /t, d/ + /l/ (*IPE* 8.05(8))—see also section 3.19 of this course for consonants + syllabic /l/.

Note: When /t, d/ are followed by /l/, the plosive is released over the sides of the tongue, without an intervening sound.

C21 *Listen*
little   middle   atlas   needless

C22 *Listen*
(1) atl   (2) at^{h}l   (3) adl   (4) ad^{ə}l
(5) atla   (6) at^{h}la   (7) adla   (8) ad^{ə}la

C23 *Identify* the items which have an intrusive [^{h}] or vowel between the plosive and /l/; check in Appendix p. 75.
bottle   model   cattle   at last   idle   badly

C24 *Listen and repeat*
medal   metal   title   tidal
gentle   handle   lately   padlock

3.10 Affricates (*IPE* 8.10–8.12)

chain   Jane   train   drain
/   tʃ   dʒ   tr   dr   /

Notes:
(a) For practical teaching purposes, /tʃ, dʒ/ should be regarded as having much in common with /tr, dr/, the important difference being that the tongue contact is more retracted for /tr, dr/.
(b) /tr, dr/ do not occur in syllable final position.
(c) /tʃ/ has the effect of shortening preceding sounds.
(d) /r/ of /tr/ is devoiced.

C25 *Listen*
chip trip Jane drain butcher aged perch purge

C26 *Identify* /tʃ, dʒ, tr, dr/ in the following items; check in Appendix p. 75.

C27 *Listen and repeat* (comparison /tʃ/—/tr/)
cheese trees chap trap chain train

C28 *Listen and repeat* (comparison /dʒ/—/dr/)
Jane drain Jew drew jug drug

3.11 Sequences /t + ʃ, t + r, d + r/

Note: When a clear sense division occurs between the syllable ending in /t/ or /d/ and the following syllable beginning with /ʃ/ or /r/, the plosive and /ʃ/ or /r/ are not affricated.

C29 *Listen and repeat*
lightship nutshell footrest handrail

3.12 Clusters: plosive or affricate + affricate

Note: Plosives before an affricate have no audible release; affricates before affricates keep their full form.

C30 *Listen and repeat*
picture object actress
black dress which cheese large trees

3.13 /tʃ, dʒ/ and /tj, dj/

C31 *Listen and repeat*
chewed tube juice deuce

C32 (recapitulation: affricates)
Listen and repeat
jaw drip choke trace judge
ridge chase draw joke rich
nature major country hundred

3.14 Fricatives (*IPE* 8.13–8.19)

fine	vine	think	this	seal	zeal	sheep	measure	how
/ f	v	θ	ð	s	z	ʃ	ʒ	h /

Notes:
  (a) The main features which distinguish the English fricatives are:
    (1) place of articulation
    (2) voicing
    (3) length of preceding sounds.
  (b) /ʒ/ occurs mainly in medial positions and only occasionally finally; very rare initially.
  (c) /h/ occurs only in syllable-initial positions.

3.15 Fricatives: place of articulation (*IPE* 8.13(1))

Notes:
  (a) The places are:
    labio-dental /f, v/ (*IPE* 8.15)
    dental /θ, ð/ (*IPE* 8.16)
    alveolar /s, z/ (*IPE* 8.17)
    palato-alveolar /ʃ, ʒ/ (*IPE* 8.18)
    glottal /h/ (*IPE* 8.19).
  (b) English has a fricative system which is more complex than that of most languages. A clear distinction between dental:alveolar:palato-alveolar is very important.

C33 *Listen*
    fin   thin   sin shin him
    clove clothe close (*vb.*) beige

C34 *Identify* the fricatives in the following items; check in Appendix p. 75.

C35 *Listen and repeat*
    sheet fine sink   this zinc   close (*vb.*)
    life   seat clothe dish think vine beige

3.16 Fricatives: voicing (*IPE* 8.13(1))

Note: Voicing (i.e. vibration of the vocal folds) is distinctive mainly in medial positions.

C36   *Listen*
surface   service   earthy   worthy
racer   razor   fission   vision

C37   *Listen and repeat*
offer   father   essay   mission   decision
over   author   easy   pleasure

3.17   Fricatives: length of preceding sounds (*IPE* 8.13(4))—see also sections 2.3, 2.7 of this course.

Note: Long vowels and diphthongs are shorter before syllable-final /f, θ, s, ʃ/ than before /v, ð, z, ʒ/, thus, as in the case of plosives, providing an important cue in the distinction of final fricatives.

C38   *Listen*
fife   five   loath   loathe
place   plays   elation   evasion

C39   *Listen and repeat*
leaf   teethe   peace   leave   pens   emotion   peas   teeth
explosion   use (*vb.*)   earthy   pence   worthy   use (*n.*)

C40   *Listen and repeat* (/v/—/b/)
vest   best   vote   boat   vowel   bowel

C41   *Listen and repeat* (/θ/—/t/)
thin   tin   thank   tank   ether   eater
heath   heat   both   boat

C42   *Listen and repeat* (/θ/—/s/)
thick   sick   thought   sort   ethics   Essex
mouth   mouse

C43   *Listen and repeat* (/ð/—/z/)
writhing   rising   breathe   breeze   clothed   closed

C44   *Listen and repeat* (/ð/—/d/)
there   dare   other   udder   breathe   breed

C45   *Listen and repeat* (/ʃ/—/tʃ/)
shoes   choose   washing   watching   dish   ditch

C46 *Listen and repeat* (/ʒ/—/dʒ/)
leisure ledger vision pigeon

C47 *Listen and repeat* (/-/—/h/)
eat heat ear hear the edge the hedge

C48 *Listen and repeat* (clusters with /s, z/ and /θ, ð/)
clothes months those three both sides
Who's that? What's the time?

3.18 Nasals (*IPE* 8.20–8.23)

sum sun sung
/ m n ŋ /

Notes:
(a) /m, n/ offer no difficulty, except that /n/ like /t, d/ is alveolar rather than dental.
(b) /ŋ/ occurs usually only after a vowel, and must be distinguished from the sequences /ŋg/ and /ŋk/. /ŋg/ occurs only before a vowel or /l/.
(c) /n/ is frequently syllabic, i.e. forms a syllable without an accompanying vowel; /m/ occurs less frequently in a syllabic form, and /ŋ/ rarely (e.g. it is made syllabic by some speakers in a word like *bacon*).

C49 *Listen*
sum sun sung sinner singer

C50 *Identify* /n/ or /ŋ/ in the following items; check in Appendix p. 75.

C51 *Listen and repeat*
sing sin hanged hand singer sinner
robbing robin

C52 *Identify* /ŋ/ or /ŋg/ or /ŋk/ in the following items; check in Appendix p. 75.

C53 *Listen and repeat*
hanger hunger singer longer longing
single finger anchor anger singing
sinking

C54   *Listen and repeat* (syllabic /n/—see also section 3.8 of this course)

cotton   sudden   often   oven   earthen
southern   listen   dozen   mission   vision

C55   *Listen and repeat* (syllabic /m/)
rhythm   prism   lissome

3.19   /l/ (*IPE* 8.24, 8.25)

Notes:

(a) Two main variants of /l/ occur in RP. It is important for the foreign learner to use these variants correctly:

(1) 'Clear' [l], with a front vowel resonance similar to the *l* sound commonly found in many languages, occurs before vowels and /j/, e.g. in *leaf, late, blow, glad, silly, sailor, million, nobly, ugly,* etc.

(2) 'Dark' [ɫ], with a back vowel resonance resembling an *o* or *u* sound, occurs in final positions, before a consonant and as a syllabic consonant, e.g. in *feel, doll, pale, oil, cold, milk, self, bills, almost, silver, apple, little, final,* etc. This 'dark' [ɫ] is articulated by placing the tongue-tip on the upper teeth ridge as for 'clear' [l] and simultaneously articulating a vowel of the *o* or *u* type with the back of the tongue. (See also section 3.9 of this course for /l/ after /t, d/.) Note, however, that the spelling *l* before a consonant is often silent, e.g. in *talk, half, salmon, folk,* etc.

(b) Another variant, a voiceless variety symbolized as [l̥], is used particularly after an accented /p/ or /k/, and is important in distinguishing the members of such pairs as *plead—bleed* or *class—glass.*

3.20   Comparison: [l] and [ɫ]

C56   *Listen* (comparison [ɫ] and [o])
ɫ   o   ɫ   o   ɫ   o

C57   *Listen* (comparison [l] and [ɫ])
l   ɫ   ɫ   l   ɫ   l   ɫ

C58   *Identify* [l] or [ɫ] in the following; check in Appendix p. 75.

C59 *Identify* [l] or [ɫ] in the following words; in some cases the wrong variant of /l/ is used; check in Appendix p. 75.
lend   laugh   told   light   ill
healthy   old   life   lake   table

C60 *Listen and repeat*
silly   feel   doll   light   million   false
cold   milk   film   apple   uncle   bottle
saddle   measles

3.21   Comparison: [l] and [l̥]

C61 *Listen*
plead   bleed   class   glass
plight blight   clue   glue

C62 *Identify* incorrect use of [l] (instead of [l̥]) in the following words; check in Appendix p. 75.
place   glad   clean   blow
plan   clear   glass   clock

C63 *Listen and repeat*
plead   glue   class   plot
clue   blot   glass   bleed

3.22   [ɫ] → [l]

Note: Word final [ɫ] may be pronounced [l] when followed by a word beginning with a vowel or /j/ in the same sense group.

C64 *Listen*
feel   feel it   all   all over   will   will you

3.23   /r/ (*IPE* 8.26)

Notes:
(a) The most common form of /r/ is a voiced frictionless continuant, made with the tip of the tongue near but not touching the rear part of the upper teeth ridge; the central part of the tongue is hollowed. It is somewhat similar to /ʒ/, but without the friction and with a more retracted articulation.

(b) Friction occurs, however, when /r/ follows /t, d/ as part of the clusters /tr, dr/ and also after /p, k/. After accented /p, t, k/, /r/ is devoiced (symbol [r̥]), and constitutes an important feature distinguishing such sequences from /br, dr, gr/, e.g. the pair *crow—grow*.

(c) /r/ is pronounced only before a vowel. Care must be taken in speaking RP not to pronounce an *r* sound in words like *far* (when followed by a pause or a consonant), *cart* or *farm*. However, *r* is normally pronounced as a linking sound finally in a word when the next word begins with a vowel and has a close syntactic association, e.g. in *far away*.

C65 *Listen*
ɑː ɑːrə ɑː ɑːrə

C66 *Identify* the non-English *r* sounds used in the following items; check in Appendix p. 75.
(1) ɑː (2) ɑː   (3) ɑːrə (4) ɑː
(5) ɑː (6) ɑːrə (7) ɑːrə (8) ɑː

C67 *Listen and repeat*
red raw road very arrive sorry

C68 *Listen and repeat* (/r/ in clusters)
free three shrink sprint street scream

C69 *Listen and repeat* (more than one /r/ in a word)
library brewery rarer bravery

C70 *Listen and repeat* (comparison [r̥]—[r])
pray bray try dry   crow grow

C71 *Listen and repeat* (comparison /tr, dr/—/tʃ, dʒ/)
train chain   drain Jane

C72 *Identify* those words in which an *r* sound is incorrectly inserted; check in Appendix p. 75.
bird here farm born
dear horse there learn

C73 *Listen and repeat* (linking /r/)
far off here and there poor old man
there are two father and mother

Note: Many RP speakers will make a similar link with /r/ even when there is no *r* in the spelling, e.g. in such cases as *the idea* (/r/) *of, China* (/r/) *and Japan*, etc. (*IPE* 8.26(3)). There is no need for the foreign learner to imitate this.

3.24 Comparison /l/ and /r/

Note: Some learners, notably speakers of Oriental languages where the opposition does not exist, have difficulty in distinguishing /l/ and /r/. It should be remembered that, in the case of /l/, contact is made between the tongue-tip and the upper teeth ridge; such a contact is not usually made for /r/. In addition, the articulation of /r/ is more retracted than that of /l/.

C74 *Listen* (comparison /l/—/r/)
 lɑː rɑː ɑːrə ɑːlə
 blɑː brɑː klɑː grɑː

C75 *Identify* /l/ or /r/ in the following items; check in Appendix p. 76.

C76 *Listen and repeat*
 right light pilot pirate pray play
 fly fry bright blight clash crash

3.25 /j/ (*IPE* 8.28)

Notes:
 (a) /j/ may be regarded as a rapidly articulated /iː/ or /ɪ/.
 (b) When /j/ follows accented /p, t, k, h/, /j/ is devoiced, e.g. in *pew, tune, cure, huge*.
 (c) Many words containing the sequence /juː/ have an alternative pronunciation without /j/ particularly after accented /l, s, z/, e.g. *salute, suit, presume* (/sə'ljuːt/ or /sə'luːt/, etc.). /juː/ is however retained after plosives, nasals, /f, v, h/ and unaccented /l/, e.g. in *beauty, new, few, huge, value*, etc.

C77 *Listen and repeat*
 you yes young Europe beauty argue new

C78 *Listen and repeat* (devoicing of /j/ after accented /p, t, k, h/)
 pure tune cure huge accuse

C79   *Listen and repeat*

/j/—/dʒ/	year	jeer	yet jet
/tj/—/tʃ/	tune	chew	
/dj/—/dʒ/	dune	June	

3.26   /w/ (*IPE* 8.29)

Notes:

(a) /w/ may be regarded as a rapidly articulated /uː/ or /ʊ/.

(b) Some learners have difficulty in distinguishing /w/ and /v/. They should practise replacing /w/ by /uː/, gradually reducing the length of /uː/, e.g. *west* /uːest/ → /west/.

(c) When /w/ follows accented /t, k/, /w/ is devoiced, e.g. in *twice, quite*.

(d) Some English speakers pronounce words beginning with *wh* (e.g. *which, why, wheat, white*, etc.) with /hw/. This usage is now rare in RP and need not be imitated by foreign learners.

C80   *Listen and repeat*
wet wasp wood one

C81   *Listen* (comparison /w/—/v/)
waː vaː wiː viː vuː wuː

C82   *Identify* /w/ or /v/ in the following items; check in Appendix p. 76.

C83   *Listen and repeat* (/w/—/v/)
west vest   wine vine   verse worse

C84   *Listen and repeat* (devoicing of /w/ after accented /t, k/)
twelve twice queen quick

C85   *Listen and repeat*
wood word wear squirrel
swim equal away language

3.27   Consonant clusters (*IPE* 9.08, 9.09)

Notes: (a) English permits a large number of consonant clusters in the word, some of which have already been practised in preceding sections. The potential structure of the monosyllable may be expressed as (CCC)V(CCCC), i.e. up to 3 consonants may precede the vowel, and up to 4 consonants may follow the vowel.

(b) Even more complex sequences may, of course, occur at word or syllable boundaries.

(c) The following drills present a selection of 3 consonant word initial clusters and of 2 or more word final clusters. The learner should avoid pronouncing any intrusive sounds between the consonants of these clusters or adding a sound before initial clusters.

C86 *Listen and repeat* (initial CCC—the first of which is always /s/; do not pronounce a vowel before /s/)
splash   spread   spume   strain
stew   scream   skewer   square

C87 *Listen and repeat* (final CC—a selection)
apt   depth   eighth   act   robbed
touched   judged   bench   range
film   fifth   waves   earthed   clothed
warmth   month   moths

C88 *Listen and repeat* (final CCC and CCCC—a selection)
lapsed   depths   next   sixth   pinched
hinged   thanked   months   twelfth   lisped
asked   prompts   texts   sixths

3.28 Consonant assimilation (*IPE* 11.04–11.08)

Notes:
(a) Learners will notice that the pronunciation of a word in connected speech may be different from that which it has when said in isolation. In particular, in ordinary colloquial speech, English speakers often change the articulation of a word final consonant in anticipation of the first consonant of the following word.

(b) *Variation of place of articulation,* e.g.
/n/ → /m/: ten‿boys
/n/ → /ŋ/: ten‿girls
/d/ → /b/: good‿boy
/s/ → /ʃ/: this‿shop

/z/ → /ʒ/: those_shops
/t+j/ → /tʃ/: Won't_you?
/d+j/ → /dʒ/: Could_you?
/s+j/ → /ʃ/: this_year
/z+j/ → /ʒ/: it was_your fault

(c) *Devoicing* (comparatively rare), e.g.

/v/ → /f/: of_course
      I have_to go
/dʒ/ → /tʃ/: Bridge_Street

(d) The foreign learner need not imitate these assimilations in his own pronunciation, but he should expect to hear them from the native English speaker.

(e) Certain types of assimilation, common in other languages, are untypical of English and should be avoided by the learner, e.g. *voicing*

/k/ → /g/: black_dress
/s/ → /z/: nice_boy
/θ/ → /ð/: birth_day
place /z/ → /ð/: I was_there

C89 *Listen* (colloquial assimilation of final consonants)

ten/m/ boys	ten/ŋ/ girls	good/b/ boy
that/k/ cat	this/ʃ/ shop	those/ʒ/ shops
won't you/tʃ/	could you/dʒ/	this/ʃ/ year
it was/ʒ/ your fault	I have/f/ to go	

C90 *Listen* (incorrect assimilations)

black/k/ dress	*not*	black/g/ dress
nice/s/ boy	*not*	nice/z/ boy
birth/θ/day	*not*	birth/ð/day
I was/z/ there	*not*	I was/ð/ there

Section 4
Accentuation and rhythm

4.1 Accentuation of the word (*IPE* 9.01–9.05)

Notes:

(a) In polysyllabic English words, one syllable carries the main (primary) accent. The situation of the primary accent varies from word to word, e.g.

on the last syllable:	*behind, result, cigarette*
on the penultimate syllable	*answer, together,*
	important
on the ante-penultimate syllable:	*yesterday, afterwards,*
	critical, etc.

If easy intelligibility is to be achieved, it is extremely important to give words their correct accentual pattern and characteristic rhythm.

(b) When a syllable is accented, it is made more prominent than its neighbours by means of any or all of four factors: stress, pitch, quality, quantity. Of these, pitch prominence, associated with stress (loudness for the listener), is the most important.

(c) It is a crucial feature of English pronunciation that syllables which are unaccented tend to have weak and obscure qualities. Thus, /ə/ and syllabic /l, m, n/ occur typically only in unaccented syllables; /ɪ, ʊ/ occur frequently in both accented and unaccented syllables. All other vowels and diphthongs (hereafter referred to as 'strong vowels') may occur in syllables other than those carrying the primary accent, but will often have a secondary degree of accent associated with them.

(d) In the drill patterns which follow, the syllable carrying the primary accent will be shown as ➘; unaccented syllables as ∙; syllables with strong vowels and secondary accent as ●; syllables with strong vowels but with weak accent as ○.

(e) In phonetic transcriptions and in ordinary orthography, accents will be shown as follows:

primary accent: '
secondary accent: ֽ
unaccented: no mark

4.2   Accentual patterns: 2-syllable words

4.2.1.   *Patterns:* . ➘, ➘ .

A1   *Listen*
 lɪˈlɪ   ˈlɪlɪ   ˈlɪlɪ   lɪˈlɪ   lɪˈlɪ   ˈlɪlɪ

A2   *Identify* the accentual patterns given for /lɪlɪ/; check in Appendix p. 76.

A3   *Listen* to the words given; transcribe them, marking the accent; check in Appendix p. 76.
annoy   armour   sofa   police   marble   below

A4   *Listen and repeat*
(. ➘)   alone   machine   behind
(➘ .)   over   under   husband

4.2.2. *Patterns:* ● ➘, ➘ ○

Notes:
(a) The patterns resemble those above, but the syllable not carrying the primary accent has a strong vowel.
(b) When the syllable containing the strong vowel precedes ➘, a secondary accent may be associated with it (●); when the syllable containing the strong vowel follows ➘, there is no secondary accent (○).

A5   *Listen*
ˈlɑːlɑː   ˌlɑːˈlɑː   ˌlɑːˈlɑː   ˈlɑːlɑː

A6   *Listen and repeat*
(● ➘)   unknown   idea   antique

A7   *Listen and repeat* (comparison . ➘ and ● ➘)
contain   canteen   ado   undo   until   untie

A8   *Listen and repeat*
(➘ ○)   female   programme   window

A9 *Listen and repeat* (comparison ❯ . and ❯ ₒ)
    never nephew   pillar pillow   hostel hostile

4.3   Accentual patterns: 3-syllable words

4.3.1 *Patterns:* ❯ . ., . ❯ .

A10 *Listen*
    ˈlaːlələ ləˈlaːlə ləˈlɪlɪ ˈlɪlɪlə

A11 *Identify* the accentual patterns of the nonsense items given; check in Appendix p. 76.

A12 *Listen* to the words given; transcribe them, marking the accent; check in Appendix p. 76.
    quality   enormous   container
    solution   luckily   character

A13 *Listen and repeat*
    (❯ . .) yesterday bachelor quantity
    (. ❯ .) important relation   eleven

4.3.2 *Patterns:* ● . ❯, ❯ . ●, ● ❯ ., . ❯ ₒ

Note: When a syllable containing a strong vowel immediately follows ❯, there is no secondary accent; in other cases, a syllable containing a strong vowel (but not carrying the primary accent) has a secondary accent.

A14 *Listen*
    ˌlaːləˈlaː ˈlaːləˌlaː ˌlaːˈlaːlə ləˈlaːlaː

A15 *Identify* the accentual patterns of the nonsense items given; check in Appendix p. 76.

A16 *Listen and repeat*
    (● . ❯) understand cigarette   afternoon
    (❯ . ●) appetite   photograph telephone
    (● ❯ .) uncertain   re-entry   .substandard
    (. ❯ ₒ) tobacco   tomato   projectile

4.4   Distinctive accentual patterns: 2-syllable words

Note: Certain 2-syllable words distinguish their noun/adjective form from their verb form by a difference of accentual pattern, the noun/adj. form having ➘ . (or ➘ o) and the verb . ➘.

4.4.1   *Distinction by stress/pitch alone:*

A17   *Listen and repeat*
'import (*n.*)   im'port (*vb*)   in'sult (*vb.*)   'insult (*n.*)

4.4.2   *Distinction by stress/pitch + changes of quality:*

A18   *Listen*
n./adj.	vb.
'frequent	fre'quent
'object	ob'ject
'present	pre'sent
'rebel	re'bel
'conduct	con'duct

A19   *Identify* the noun/adjective or verb forms of the words given; check in Appendix p. 76.
(1) present   (2) object   (3) conduct   (4) rebel
(5) present   (6) rebel   (7) conduct   (8) object

A20   *Listen and repeat*
subject (*vb.*)   present (*adj.*)   record (*n.*)
convict (*n.*)   conduct (*vb.*)   perfect (*adj.*)
refuse (*vb.*)   object (*vb.*)   refuse (*n.*)

Note: Some 2-syllable words do not follow this general rule, or show signs of instability, e.g.:
   comment has ➘ o /'kɒment/ for both noun and verb
   contact has ➘ o /'kɒntækt/ for the noun, and ➘ o or . ➘ /ˌkɒn'tækt/ for the verb
   dispute has . ➘ for both noun and verb, but increasingly ➘ o /'dɪspjuːt/ is used for the noun.

4.5   Distinctive accentual patterns: 3- or 4-syllable words

Note: Some words of 3 or more syllables also show distinctive accentual patterns in their noun/adjective and verb forms:

(a) with a shift of the primary accent and associated sound changes

(b) with the primary accent constant, but with sound changes.

A21 *Listen and repeat*

		n./adj.	*vb.*
(a)	alternate	/ˌɔːlˈtɜːnət	ˈɔːltəˌneɪt/
	envelope	/ˈenvəˌləʊp	ɪnˈveləp/
	attribute	/ˈætrɪˌbjuːt	əˈtrɪbjuːt/
(b)	associate	/əˈsəʊʃɪət	əˈsəʊʃɪˌeɪt/
	compliment	/ˈkɒmplɪmənt	ˈkɒmplɪˌment/
	separate	/ˈsepərət	ˈsepəˌreɪt/
	prophesy	/ˈprɒfəsɪ	ˈprɒfɪˌsaɪ/

4.6 Accentual patterns: 4-syllable words

A22 *Identify* the accentual patterns of the nonsense items given; check in Appendix p. 76.

A23 *Listen and repeat*
(. ➘ . .) remarkable impossible photography

A24 *Listen and repeat*
(• ➘ . .) unfortunate rhinoceros subliminal

A25 *Listen and repeat*
(• . ➘ .) unimportant photographic circulation

A26 *Listen and repeat*
(. ➘ . •) acclimatize negotiate solidify

A27 *Listen and repeat*
(➘ . . .) caterpillar criticism melancholy

A28 *Listen and repeat*
(➘ . • .) educated helicopter prophesying

A29 *Listen and repeat*
(➘ . . •) capitalize counterattack

A30 *Listen and repeat*
(• . . ➘) superimpose aquamarine

4.7   Recapitulation: 2- to 4-syllable words

A31   *Listen and repeat* (transcriptions with accentual patterns are given in Appendix p. 76).

enumerate	thirteen	constipated	alone
invitation	paragraph	under	automobile
Morocco	sub-normal	searchlight	superintend

4.8   Accentual patterns: 5- to 8-syllable words (a selection)

A32   (*5 syllables*)
Listen and repeat

(＼ . . . .)	capitalism	cannibalism
(. ＼ . . .)	administrative	catholicism
(. • . ＼ .)	consideration	apotheosis
(• . ＼ . .)	objectivity	aristocracy
(• . ＼ . •)	incapacitate	inexactitude
(• . . ＼ .)	counterproductive	interdependence

A33   (*6 syllables*)
Listen and repeat

(. • . ＼ . .)	inferiority	impossibility
(• . . ＼ . .)	variability	meteorological
(• . ＼ . . .)	ceremoniously	indistinguishable
(• . . . ＼ .)	onomatopeic	palatalization
(. • . . ＼ .)	personification	electrification

A34   (*7, 8 syllables*)
Listen and repeat

(. • . . ＼ . .)	intelligibility
(• . ＼ . . . .)	unilateralism
(. • . . . ＼ .)	industrialization
(• . • . . . ＼ .)	internationalization

4.9   Suffixation and accentuation

Note: The word accentual pattern is determined by the type of certain suffixes. The following is a selection of common types of suffix which attract the primary accent of the base word, with frequent qualitative changes.

4.9.1 *Attracting the primary accent to the penultimate:*

A35 (*Suffix -ial* /-ɪəl/)
Listen and repeat
proverb proverbial colony colonial
tutor tutorial

A36 (*Suffix -ian* /-ɪən/)
Listen and repeat
civil civilian comedy comedian
grammar grammarian Canada Canadian

A37 (*Suffix -ic* /-ɪk/)
Listen and repeat
atom atomic drama dramatic strategy strategic

A38 (*Suffix -ion* /-(ə)n/)
Listen and repeat
communicate communication operate operation
supervise supervision execute execution

4.9.2 *Attracting the primary accent to the antepenultimate:*

A39 (*Suffix -ity* /-ətɪ/)
Listen and repeat
captive captivity curious curiosity
final finality inferior inferiority

4.10 Compound words (*IPE* 9.03)

Note: The accentual patterning of compounds is as significant as that of simple words. The most common type of compound accentuation has a primary accent on the first element.

4.10.1 *2-syllable compounds:*

(1) In a few words, the weaker element undergoes an obscuration of vowel quality giving a pattern ↘ ..

A40 *Listen and repeat*
(↘ .) postman chairman saucepan

(2) More frequently, the vowel of the second element remains strong, giving a pattern   ╲ ○ .

A41   *Listen and repeat*
(╲ ○)   cardboard   earthquake
windscreen   teapot

(3) Other, less numerous 2-syllable compounds carry the primary accent on the second element, the first element having a secondary accent.

A42   *Listen and repeat*
(• ╲)   downstairs   full-grown
mince-pie   first-class

4.10.2   *3-syllable compounds:*

Again, either the first or the second element may carry the primary accent.[1]

A43   *Listen and repeat*
(╲ • .)   grasshopper   grandfather   newspaper

A44   *Listen and repeat*
(╲ . •)   buttonhole   chambermaid   honeymoon

A45   *Listen and repeat*
(• ╲ .)   archbishop   blackcurrant   field-marshal

A46   *Listen and repeat*
(• . ╲)   country-house   gingerbeer   second-hand

4.10.3   *4- or 5-syllable compounds:*

(1) *4-syllables*

A47   *Listen and repeat*
(╲ . • •)   booking-office   season-ticket
(╲ . . •)   musical-box   catherine-wheel
(. ╲ • •)   despatch-rider   machine-minder
(• . ╲ .)   easy-going   indiarubber
(• ╲ . .)   vice-chancellor   postgraduate

---

[1] When the second element of a compound is a polysyllable, it may carry a full secondary accent even though it immediately follows the primary accent.

(2) *5-syllables*

A48 *Listen and repeat*
(↘ . • .) fire-extinguisher
(↘ . • .) cabinet-maker
(• ↘ . • .) hot-water-bottle

A49 *Listen and repeat* (a selection of different compound patterns)
chatterbox   shop-window   free-wheel   washstand
power-station   mass-production   waiting-room

4.11 Compounds and noun phrases
Note: The accentual patterns of compounds must be distinguished from those of noun phrases (*adj.+n.* or *n.+n.*), which have typically a secondary accent + primary accent.

A50 *Listen and repeat* (comparison: noun phrase and compound)
noun phrase		*compound*	
a black bird	(. • ↘)	a blackbird	(. ↘ o)
a light ship	(. • ↘)	a lightship	(. ↘ o)
a cross word	(. • ↘)	a crossword	(. ↘ o)
a grand father	(. • ↘ .)	a grandfather	(. ↘ • .)

Note: In place names, such words as *Road*, *Square* (e.g. *Euston Road*) carry a primary accent; *Street* is either unaccented with a strong vowel (e.g. *North Street*— ↘ o) or carries a secondary accent (e.g. *Oxford Street*— ↘ . •).

4.12 Variation of word accentual patterns (*IPE* 11.03)

Note: Words carrying more than one accent may exhibit a weakening of the primary accent when used attributively (i.e. they are affected by the larger accentual/rhythmic context).

A51 *Listen and repeat*
thirteen   (• ↘)   thirteen pounds (• o ↘)
afternoon (• . ↘)   afternoon tea   (• . • ↘)

4.13 Accentuation in connected speech (*IPE* 10.01–10.04)
Notes:
   (a) Variations of accentual prominence, similar to those found in words, also occur in connected speech. The main accented syllables tend to occur at roughly equal intervals of time, giving the utterance a strongly rhythmical nature.
   (b) Unlike the accentual patterns of words, which are generally unalterable, the accented words of a sentence may be varied according to the sense, as may be the situation of the primary accent (see also section 5, *Intonation*).
   (c) However, the words which are most likely to carry a strong accent are those which are most important for the meaning, e.g. verbs, adverbs, nouns, adjectives (*lexical* items or *content* words). Other, *grammatical* words (often called *form* words) such as articles, prepositions, pronouns, auxiliary verbs, etc., tend to be unaccented. Thus, typically, in 'He wants a cup of tea', 'wants, cup, tea' attract strong accents, whereas 'he, a, of' are unaccented and have their quality very much obscured. Note, however, that grammatical words may often carry a strong accent when appropriate to the sense. Thus, 'he' in the above sentence may be strongly accented when an opposition with, for instance, 'she' is intended.

4.14 Types of rhythmic groups
Note: Alternations of strong and weak syllables, similar to those found in words, may also occur in connected speech.

4.14.1 Alternation weak and strong syllables:

A52 *Listen and repeat*
   (. ➘)   the man   a dog   at last   of course

A53 *Listen and repeat*
   (➘ .)   take them   can it   leave us

A54 *Listen and repeat*
   (. ➘ .)   at Christmas   an apple   the table

A55 *Listen and repeat*
   (• . ➘)   six fifteen   this alone   leave it there

A56 *Identify* the accented syllables in the following sentences; check in Appendix p. 76.
(1) Of course we want to come.
(2) The children like to run about.
(3) That's the way to do it.
(4) He couldn't come on Tuesday night
(5) She came in time for tea.

Listen again and repeat the sentences in **A56**.

Additional practice drills (not recorded):
Tra'falgar 'Square.
We 'thought you'd 'gone a'broad.
'When you 'get to 'London, 'take a 'taxi.
'All the 'women 'wore their 'summer 'dresses.

4.14.2   *2 intervening weak syllables:*

A57 *Listen and repeat*
$(. . \searrow)$ the police   a machine   it depends

A58 *Listen and repeat*
$(\searrow . .)$ look at it   wait for them   come with us

A59 *Identify* the accented syllables in the following sentences; check in Appendix p. 76.
(1) It was all we could find.
(2) Everyone thought it was terrible.
(3) There was one of the books on the table.
(4) When we arrived, it was dark.

Listen again and repeat the sentences in **A59**.

Additional practice drills (not recorded):
'What did you 'put in it?
The po'lice had a'rrested the 'culprits.
In the 'summer, the 'colours are 'wonderful.
In a 'way, it's a 'blessing for 'all of them.

4.14.3   *3 or more intervening syllables:*

A60   *Identify* the accented syllables in the following sentences; check in Appendix p. 77.
(1) A hundred and eleven.
(2) How can it be proved?
(3) Some of us were surprised.
(4) See if you can find it in the kitchen.

Listen again and repeat the sentences in **A60**.

Additional practice drills (not recorded):
It was the 'only one he could 'find.
'Then there was a 'deafening ex'plosion.
The 'quality of the 'candidates was de'plorable.

4.14.4   *Juxtaposed strong syllables:*

A61   *Listen and repeat*
(● ↘) not now   how long   good luck

A62   *Listen and repeat*
(● ● ↘) Can John come?   two black pens

A63   *Listen and repeat*
(● ● ● ↘)   Why can't Jack go?   Most men like dogs.

4.14.5   *Irregular combinations of strong and weak syllables:*

Note: Make sure that the strong syllables occur at roughly equal intervals of time, the degree of compression of the weak syllables depending upon their number.

A64   *Identify* the accented syllables in the following sentences; check in Appendix p. 77.
(1) It's all very well.
(2) He gave us ten days' notice.
(3) It's no good crying over spilt milk.

Listen again and repeat the sentences in **A64**.

Additional practice drills (not recorded):
It's 'that 'big 'house over 'there.
When 'Mary 'got 'back 'home, she 'found the 'door 'locked.
'Some 'people 'thought 'John 'Brown had 'won.

4.14.6 *Expanding sentence:*
Note: The basic sentence *the car stopped* (. • ↘) is expanded to give changing rhythmic patterns.

A65 *Listen and repeat*
The 'car 'stopped.
And the 'car 'stopped.
The 'black 'car 'stopped.
The 'car in 'front 'stopped.
The 'car 'stopped 'suddenly.
The 'car had 'almost 'stopped.
The 'car be'hind 'stopped at the 'corner.

4.15 Weak and strong forms (*IPE* 10.04)

Notes:
(a) As has been mentioned, it is important to weaken and obscure those grammatical words which may be totally unaccented. If such words are pronounced with their full forms when unaccented, a serious loss of intelligibility for the English listener may result. Thus, 'We have come for the books' is less easy to understand when pronounced /wiː hæv kʌm fɔː ðiː bʊks/ than if it is pronounced /wiːv kʌm fə ðə bʊks/.

A66 *Listen*
/wiː hæv kʌm fɔː ðiː bʊks   wiːv 'kʌm fə ðə 'bʊks/

(b) The words most commonly reduced in this way are: *a am an and are as at be been but can could should would do does for from had has have he her him his is me must not of shall she some than that the them these to us was we will who whose you*
(c) In ordinary colloquial English, these words occur much more frequently in their weak forms than in their accented forms. Thus, *at, of, the, to, as, and, a, his, an, but, been, for, her, we, shall, was, then, them* are found to occur in their weak form in over 90 per cent of occurrences.
(d) However, all words having weak forms are said with the strong form when spoken in isolation, and may be given the strong form in cases where a special meaning related to strong accentuation is involved. In the following examples, weak and strong forms are illustrated.

4.16   Words usually weak (strong form in brackets)

a—/ə/(/eɪ/);   an—/(ə)n/(/æn/);
and—/(ə)n(d)/(/ænd/);   as—/əz/(/æz/);
but—/bət/(/bʌt/);   than—/ð(ə)n/(/ðæn/);
that (*rel. pron.* or *conj.*)—/ðət/(/ðæt/);
the—/ðɪ + V, ðə + C/(/ðiː/).

A67   *Listen and repeat* (weak)[1]
'John 'ate an 'apple and a 'pear.
'George is 'older than 'Mary, but the 'same 'age as 'Pat.
'This is the 'only 'one that I 'found.
'John 'said that 'Mary ˌtook it.

A68   *Listen and repeat* (occasional strong forms when accented)
'John 'and /ænd/ ˌMary ˌcame (i.e. insisting that *both* came)
'As /æz/ the 'car 'drew 'near ('the crowd began cheering'—
possible rhythmic accent on initial 'As')
'This is 'the /ðiː/ ˌMr ˌJones (accented 'the' implying the
'special, famous')

4.17   Prepositions usually weak (but with strong forms contrastively accented, when final or when followed by a weak pronoun)

at—/ət/(/æt/);   for—/fə(r)/(/fɔː(r)/);
from—/frəm/(/frɒm/);   of—/əv/(/ɒv/).
to—/t + Vʊ, tə + C/(/tuː/).

A69   *Listen and repeat* (weak)
'Look at 'Mary.
'This is for 'Alice, and 'this is for 'me.
He 'took it from 'John.
It's 'made of 'wood.
'Jane 'went to 'London and to Aber'deen.

A70   *Listen and repeat* (strong when contrastively accented)
'Not 'at /æt/ ˌLondon, 'in ˌLondon.
I 'voted 'for /fɔː/ the ˌmotion.
He ˌsaid 'of /ɒv/, 'not 'in.
She's 'coming 'to /tuː/ ˌLondon, 'not 'from /frɒm/ ˌLondon.

[1] Primary sentence accents are shown with '; secondary accents with ˌ.

A71 *Listen and repeat* (strong when final)
'What are you 'looking at /æt/?
'What's 'that for /fɔː/?
'Where does it 'come from /frɒm/?
'What's it 'made of /ɒv/?
'Where's 'Jack ˌgoing to /tuː/?

A72 *Listen and repeat* (optionally strong when before a weak pronoun)
'Look at /æt/ me.
He 'kept it for /fɔː/ me.
She 'took it from /frɒm/ me.
He 'found 'ten of /ɒv/ them.
'Give it to /tuː/ me.

4.18 **Forms most often weak** (but having the strong form when accented or final; 'us, them' do not have a strong form when final and unaccented)

am—/(ə)m/(/æm/);   are—/ə(r)/(/ɑː(r)/);
can—/kən/(/kæn/);   could—/kəd/(/kʊd/);
should—/ʃəd/(/ʃʊd/);   would—/(w)əd/(/wʊd/);
does—/dəz/(/dʌz/);   is—/s, z/(/ɪz/ when accented or final and also after /s, z, ʃ, ʒ, tʃ, dʒ/);
must—/məst/(/mʌst/); not—/nt/(/nɒt/);   shall—/ʃl/(/ʃæl/);
them—/ð(ə)m/(/ðem/);   us—/əs/(/ʌs/); was—/wəz/(/wɒz/);
were—/wə(r)/(/wɜː(r)/);   will—/l/(/wɪl/);
had (*aux.*)—/(h)əd/(/hæd/);
has (*aux.*)—/s, z/—/əz/ after /s, z, tʃ, dʒ, ʃ, ʒ/(/hæz/);
have (*aux.*)—/(hə)v/—/(h)əv/ after C (/hæv/)

A73 *Listen and repeat* (weak)
I'm 'coming.   The 'boys are 'here, but the 'girls are 'out.
I can 'see it.   They could 'come to'morrow.
I'd (= would) 'like it.
'Jack would 'like it, and 'so would 'they.
'Sarah should be 'here.   'What does it 'cost?
'John's 'here, and 'Jack's 'there.   'Mary must 'go.
I 'couldn't 'come.   'I shall 'come. I 'want them 'now.
He 'told us to 'come.   'Mark was 'there.   They were 'late.

They were 'all 'late.   'Jack will 'come.
The 'boys had 'found it.   They'd 'found it.
'Jack's (=has) 'found it.   'John's (=has) 'found it.
'Alice has 'gone.   I've 'lost it.   I 'must have 'lost it.

A74 *Listen and repeat* (strong when contrastively accented)
I 'am /æm/ ,coming.   'Am /æm/ I?
The ,boys 'are /ɑː/ ,here.   'Are /ɑː/ they?
I 'can /kæn/ ,see it.   They ,said they 'could /kʊd/ ,come.
I 'would /wʊd/ ,like it.   He 'should /ʃʊd/ be 'there.
,What 'does /dʌz/ it ,cost?   ,John 'is /ɪz/ ,there.
We 'must /mʌst/ ,go.   'Must /mʌst/ we 'go?
He's 'not /nɒt/ 'coming.   I 'shall /ʃæl/ ,go.
'Shall /ʃæl/ I 'go?   I ,want 'them /ðem/ to ,have it.
She'd ,like 'us /ʌs/ to ,come.   I 'was /wɒz/ ,there.
'Was /wɒz/ he 'there?   He 'will /wɪl/ ,come.
'Will /wɪl/ he 'come?   They 'were /wɜː/ ,late.
'Were /wɜː/ they 'late?   They 'had /hæd/ ,seen it.
'Had /hæd/ they 'seen it?   We 'have /hæv/ ,got it.
'Have /hæv/ you 'got it?   He 'has /hæz/ ,come.
'Has /hæz/ he 'come?

A75 *Listen and repeat* (strong when final, unaccented)
He's 'taller than 'I am /æm/.   I 'think 'they are /ɑː/.
I'll 'see if 'John can /kæn/.   They 'said 'they could /kʊd/.
I 'thought 'I would /wʊd/.   I 'think 'he should /ʃʊd/.
'See if 'he does /dʌz/.   She 'told us 'he is /ɪz/.
'John must /mʌst/.   I 'thought not /nɒt/.
I 'think 'I shall /ʃæl/.   'Yes, 'he was /wɒz/.
I 'don't ,think 'John will /wɪl/.   I 'said 'she had /hæd/.
'Yes, 'Joan had /hæd/.
'I've ,saved 'more than 'you have /hæv/.
'You were 'later than 'we were /wɜː/.

4.19 Loss of /h/ in weak forms

Note: Pronouns with initial /h/ commonly lose /h/ when they
occur unaccented within a sense group; they retain /h/ when they
are initial in a group or when they are accented (for loss of /h/ in
aux. *had, has, have,* see section 4.18 of this course). Usually affected
are: *he, his, him, her, who.*

A76 *Listen and repeat* (medial, initial and accented pronouns)
He /hiː/ 'said he /iː/ 'would. I ,said 'he /hiː/ did.
'What's his /ɪz/ 'name? His /hɪz/ 'name's 'John.
'This is 'his /hɪz/ ,book. 'Give him /ɪm/ the 'money.
,Give 'him /hɪm/ the ,money. I 'gave her /ɜː, ə/ the 'pen.
I ,gave 'her /hɜːr/ a ,pen. Her /hə/ 'father's 'here.
'He's the ,one who /uː/ ,told me. 'Who /huː/ 'told you?
I ,can't ,think 'who /huː/ it was.

4.20 Shortening of vowel in weak forms

Note: The long vowels /iː, uː, ɜː/ are optionally shortened and re-laxed when grammatical words are unaccented, e.g. /iː/ → /ɪ/ in *be, been, me, he, she, we*; /uː/ → /ʊ/ in *do* (aux.), *you*; /ɜː/ → /ə/ in *her* (see section 4.19). For reduced forms of *the*, see section 4.16; for those of *to*, see section 4.17. Often, however, the vowel, though shortened, remains tense.

A77 *Listen and repeat* (/iː/ → /ɪ/)
'I'll be /bɪ/ 'there. I'll 'be /biː/ ,there. It 'can't be /bɪ/.
'John's been /bɪn/ 'working.
'Where have you 'been /biːn/? I 'think she /ʃɪ/ 'can.
He ,said 'she /ʃiː/ can. 'What can we /wɪ/ 'do?
'What can 'we /wiː/ ,do? 'John 'gave me /mɪ/ a 'book.
,Give 'me /miː/ the ,book.

A78 *Listen and repeat* (/uː/ → /ʊ/)
Note: Aux. *do* also has a common weak form /də/.
'What do /dʊ/ we 'owe you? 'What do /də/ they 'want?
You /jʊ/ 'don't, 'do /duː/ you /jʊ/?
He 'told you /jʊ/ he 'could.
'Can you /jʊ/ 'come? Can 'you /juː/ ,come?

4.21 Special cases

4.21.1 'Some':

Note: 'Some' is pronounced:
(1) /s(ə)m/ when an unaccented determiner, e.g. 'I've 'got some 'money';

(2) /sʌm/ when an accented determiner, e.g. 'I've 'got 'some 'money (but not much); or 'I 'read it in 'some 'book' (i.e. 'I'm not sure of the name of the book');

(3) /sʌm/ when a pronoun, e.g. "I've 'got some' (unaccented); or "Some of them are 'here' (accented).

A79 *Listen and repeat*
'Would you 'like some /səm/ 'more?
I've 'got 'some /sʌm/ 'money, but 'not 'much.
'Could you 'give me some /sʌm/?

4.21.2 *'There':*

Note: 'There' is pronounced:

(1) /ðə(r)/ when used as an unaccented existential subject, e.g. 'There's /ðəz/ 'nothing, 'is there /ðə/?'; 'There /ðər/ are a 'lot of them.';

(2) /ðɛə(r)/ when an adverb, e.g. 'It's 'there /ðɛə/'.

A80 *Listen and repeat*
There /ðə/ ˌmust be 'thousands.
Is there /ðər/ 'anyone 'in?   'There /ðɛər/ it 'is!
I 'put it 'there /ðɛə/.

4.22 **Accentuation in connected speech: recapitulation**

A81 *Write* the following sentences in phonetic transcription, using the weak forms appropriate to the accentuation shown; check in Appendix p. 77.

(1) They were the 'first to a'rrive at the 'entrance.
(2) 'What are you 'going to 'bring us from 'London?
(3) He was 'waiting at the 'corner for an 'hour.
(4) I 'told them that there was a 'lot of it a'bout.
(5) 'Jack's 'not 'sure if he can 'come.
(6) 'Can I 'get to the 'Strand by 'bus?
(7) I 'thought he would 'get 'more 'votes than he 'did.

Now listen and repeat the sentences in **A81**.

Additional drills (not recorded)
Transcribe the following sentences and compare your version with that given in Appendix p. 77.

(1) He could have bought some of them, if he had had a basket.

(2) As far as I know, we won't be there till ten.
(3) What shall we do if John's late?
(4) About when does he expect to arrive?
(5) I thought there were some marvellous players there.

Section 5
Intonation

5.1 Intonation: its nature and function (*IPE* 10.10–10.30)[1]

Notes:

(a) The spoken form of language consists not only of variations in sounds and in accentual/rhythmic patterns, but also of significant changes in the musical pitch of the voice. In some 'tone' languages, e.g. many Oriental and African languages, a pitch feature distinguishes the meaning of words. In English and most European languages, the chief function of pitch variation is related to the whole utterance, which may consist of one or more words. Such 'intonation' carries important information of an accentual, grammatical or attitudinal kind. Some of these pitch signals occur with the same general meaning in all languages which make use of intonation, e.g. a falling pitch pattern is generally indicative of finality such as is associated with statements, whereas a rising pattern is related to non-finality as in non-final clauses or questions.

(b) English, however, makes certain specific uses of pitch change, both in connection with the characteristic accentual system of the language and also with regard to the meaning carried by particular types of pitch pattern, e.g. the English distinction between a falling as opposed to a falling-rising pitch pattern, which occurs comparatively rarely in other languages. It is important for the learner to identify the English pitch patterns which differ markedly from those of his own language. But it must be remembered that a given sentence cannot be said to have a single appropriate pitch pattern, nor can an intonation pattern be said to have in itself only one possible meaning: the appropriateness of an intonation pattern for any sentence will depend on (1) the accentual meaning, (2) the grammatical type

---

[1] A much fuller treatment of English intonation for foreign learners is contained in J. D. O'Connor and G. F. Arnold, *Intonation of Colloquial English* (second edition, London, Longman, 1973).

of sentence, (3) the attitude of the speaker and (4) the general
and (more specifically) the intonational context.

(c) The following sections illustrate the form and function of the
more common English intonation patterns.

5.2 The accentual form and function

Note: In the previous section, it was pointed out that in connected
English speech there is an alternation of weak and strong syllables
which gives the utterance a characteristic rhythmic beat. In any
sentence, however, one word is given more information prominence that the others, and this prominence is signalled by initiating
a 'change of pitch direction' (a falling or a rising movement) on
the accented syllable. This primary (or tonic) pitch change is
known as the 'nucleus' of the intonation group, and the type of
pitch change involved is called the 'nuclear tone'. If no special
prominence is to be associated with any word in the sentence, such
a nucleus will occur on the last accented syllable.

I 1 *Listen* (In these examples, the nucleus is shown by ⋆ before
the syllable initiating the pitch movement, the remaining
accented syllables being indicated by •.

⋆John •likes •fish.
•John ⋆likes •fish.
•John •likes ⋆fish.
Is •Mary •coming to⋆day?
Is ⋆Mary •coming to•day?
Is •Mary ⋆coming to•day?

I 2 *Identify* the place of the nucleus in the following sentences;
check in Appendix p. 77.
(1) This is my book.
(2) This is my book.
(3) This is my book.
(4) This is my book.
(5) Are you coming?
(6) Are you coming?
(7) Are you coming?
(8) I don't want any tea.
(9) I don't want any tea.
(10) I don't want any tea.

I 3   *Listen and repeat* (giving the main prominence to the syllables marked with ★ and imitating the pitch change involved).
●Do you ★want it?
Do ★you ●want it?
●Susan ●couldn't ★go.
★Susan ●couldn't ●go.
●Which ho●tel are you ★staying at?
★Which ho●tel are you ●staying at?
●Which ho★tel are you ●staying at?

5.3   Several changes of pitch direction

Note: It often happens that more than one word carries a shift of pitch direction, though the main accentual prominence is still associated with one of them.

I 4   *Listen*
(1) ★John ●likes ★fish.
(2) ★John ●likes ★fish.
(3) ★I don't ●want any ★tea.
(4) ★Which ho●tel are you ★staying at?

I 5   *Identify* the syllables initiating a pitch change; check in Appendix p. 77.
(1) This is my book.
(2) How many stamps has John got?
(3) Susan was there.
(4) Do you want it?
(5) That isn't very nice.

I 6   *Listen and repeat* (imitating the pitch changes)
★Mary ●wouldn't do ★that.
We ★wanted to ★leave in the ★morning.
★That's the ●way to ★do it.
★I wouldn't have ★let him ●do it.
★When did you ●say he ★came?

5.4   Types of nuclear tone

Note: The chief forms of pitch change (tones) associated with the nucleus are as follows:

(1) *Low fall* (marked with ͵)—fall from mid to low

(2) *High fall* (marked with ˋ)—fall from high to low

(3) *Low rise* (marked with ͵)—rise from low to mid

(4) *High rise* (marked with ´)—rise from mid to high

(5) *Fall-rise* (marked with ˅)—fall with rise

(For the Rise-fall nucleus (ˆ), which may often be regarded as a reinforcement of the High fall, see section 5.21 of this course.)

5.5   Nucleus on one syllable (with a long vowel)

I 7   *Listen* to the five basic tones on *No*.
(1) ͵No   (2) ˋNo   (3) ͵No   (4) ´No   (5) ˅No

I 8   *Identify* the nuclear tones used on the following 10 versions of *No*; check in Appendix p. 77.

I 9   *Listen and repeat* the following tones used on *No*.
(1) ͵No   (2) ˋNo   (3) ´No   (4) ͵No   (5) ´No   (6) ˅No
(7) ͵No   (8) ˋNo   (9) ˅No   (10) ͵No   (11) ˅No   (12) ͵No

5.6   Nucleus on one syllable (with a short vowel)

Note: In the case of syllables containing a short vowel, the pitch movement must be accomplished more rapidly, the extent of the movement often being reduced.

I 10   *Listen and repeat* the following tones on *Yes*.
(1) ͵Yes   (2) ˋYes   (3) ˅Yes   (4) ´Yes
(5) ͵Yes   (6) ˅Yes   (7) ˋYes   (8) ͵Yes

5.7 Unaccented syllables before the nucleus

Note: These are very often on a relatively low pitch.

I 11 *Identify* the nuclear tones used on the following items; check in Appendix p. 77.
(1) It's mine. (2) There were two. (3) You're late.
(4) He's alone? (5) A balloon! (6) It's not.
(7) Perhaps. (8) I'm surprised.

I 12 *Listen and repeat*
re'turn but it's ᵛnot at the ‚time
to'day from a ma‚chine it's a'llowed
for a ‚while

5.8 Unaccented syllables after the nucleus

Note: The realization of the basic nuclear tones is spread over the nuclear syllable and the unaccented syllables which follow, especially when a short nuclear syllable is involved, e.g. in *Listen.* Thus:

(1) ˎ = ﹍ or ﹍

(2) ˋ = ﹍ or ﹍

(3) ˏ = ﹍ or ﹍

(4) ´ = ﹍ or ﹍

(5) ᵛ = ﹍ or when more than one unaccented syllable

follows, e.g. in *Yesterday* ﹍

I 13 *Listen and repeat*
(1) ˋListen (2) ‚Listen (3) ˎListen (4) ´Listen
(5) ᵛListen

I 14 *Listen and repeat*
(1) ˎYesterday (2) ‚Yesterday (3) ᵛYesterday
(4) ˋYesterday (5) ´Yesterday

I 15 *Identify* the nuclear tones used in the following items; check in Appendix p. 77.

(1) Tomorrow   (2) It's Saturday.   (3) We expected it.
(4) She told him to.   (5) He wanted to.

I 16 *Listen and repeat*
But there were ˈtwo of them.
Can you ʹcarry it?
Does it ˌmatter?
It's ˅comfortable.
He's a ˎbachelor.

5.9 Divided fall + rise nucleus

Note: A distinction should be made between a fall-rise nucleus on one word, e.g. '˅No', or '˅Yesterday', or on more than one word when unaccented syllables follow the nucleus, e.g. 'We'll ˅wait for them' and a fall followed by a rise when both elements have accentual prominence, e.g. 'Come along'. In the latter case, the elements are marked with ˋ followed by ˌ, e.g. 'ˋCome aˌlong'.

I 17 *Listen and repeat*
ˋCome aˌlong.
ˋYou can ˌsee.
ˋBring me a ˌcup.
It ˋdoesn't ˌmatter.

I 18 *Listen and repeat* (fall + rise in adjacent clauses)
They'd aˋrrived when we ˌgot there.
He ˋsaid you wouldn't ˌlike it.
On ˋTuesday, if you ˌcan.

5.10 Accented syllables before the nucleus

Notes:
(a) Accented syllables before the nucleus may be generally high or generally low. If they are high, they often show a lively or interested attitude; if they are low, they may give a perfunctory or grudging impression.
(b) High accented syllables occurring in this pre-nuclear position are marked with ʹ; if there are more than one, they will be realized with a gradual descent of pitch levels.
(c) Low accented syllables before the nucleus are marked with ˌ.

I 19 *Listen*
(high pre-nuclear accented syllables)

He 'wasn't 'very ˌlate

(low pre-nuclear accented syllables)

He ˌwasn't ˌvery ˌlate

I 20 *Identify* the general pitch level of the accented syllables before the nucleus in the following items; check in Appendix p. 78.
(1) He wasn't very late.
(2) It can't be helped.
(3) He wasn't very late.
(4) Can you come tomorrow?
(5) It doesn't take long.
(6) Two of them didn't answer.

I 21 *Listen and repeat*
It's 'not what 'I exᵛpected.
He ˌwasn't ˌvery ˌlate.
'Come ˌin.
ˌWhen do you ˌthink he's ᵛcoming?
It 'can't be ˌhelped.
'Will you 'bring me a 'book from the ˌlibrary?
Are they ˌall ˌcoming at the ˌsame ᵛtime?

5.11 Falls before the nucleus

Note: When special emphasis is placed upon accented syllables before the nucleus, they may carry a falling tone (or, more rarely, a rising tone—see section 5.22 of this course). Falling syllables before the nucleus are marked ˋ. However, the final falling or rising tone of the group remains the nuclear tone, having the primary accent.

I 22 *Listen*
ˋThese were the ˋonly ˋgrapes I could ˋfind.

I 23 *Listen and repeat* (level and falling tones on accented syllables before the nucleus)

(1) 'These were the 'only 'grapes I could ˏfind.
(2) ˋThese were the ˋonly ˋgrapes I could ˋfind.
(3) ˏThese were the ˏonly ˏgrapes I could ˋfind.
(4) ˋThese were the ˋonly ˋgrapes I could ˇfind.

5.12 Secondary accents between ˋ and ˏ

Note: When secondary accents occur between ˋ and ˏ, they remain on a low level and are marked ˏ.

I 24 *Listen*

ˋMary's ˏcoming ˏhome toˏnight.

I 25 *Listen and repeat*

ˋCome and ˏsee if you can ˏshut it.
It ˋisn't ˏlikely to ˏrain.
ˋThat's ˏnot the ˏway to ˏdo it.

5.13 Secondary accents after the nucleus

Note: When syllables having a secondary accent (marked with ˏ) occur after the nucleus
(1) after a fall, they remain low, e.g.

I ˋwant to ˏdo it ˏnow

(2) after a rise, they continue the rise, e.g.

'Did you ˏsee him on ˏMonday?

(3) in a fall-rise (ˇ), the rise will begin on the syllable carrying the secondary accent (compare, however, section 5.9 for fall + rise), e.g.

It ˋwasn't ˏvery ˇappeˏtizing.

I 26 *Listen and repeat*

I ˋwant to ˏdo it ˏnow.
'Did you ˏsee him on ˏMonday?
ˏI didn't ˏthink it was ˏfunny!
I'm ˋsure he'll ˇteleˏphone.

I 27　*Listen* to the following passage and mark the intonation used; check in Appendix p. 78.

Where's the telephone directory?

I want John's phone number.

How is it he spells his surname?

There's an 'e' at the end of Browne, isn't there?

Here it is.　348 6287.

Is that you, John?

Oh, Mrs Browne!

I quite thought it was John.

Is he likely to be home soon?

I wanted to have a word with him about my new tape-recorder.

It's probably my fault, but I can't seem to get it to work.

Listen to the passage again and repeat it group by group

5.14　Sentence-types and attitudinal function

Notes:

(a) As well as serving to make prominent the accented words in an utterance, intonation may also distinguish different types of sentence and different attitudes of the speaker.

(b) In the following sections, examples will be given of such sentence-types as:

    (1) statements

    (2) WH questions (i.e. questions beginning with such words as 'when, why', etc.)

    (3) Yes/No questions (i.e. questions expecting the answer 'yes' or 'no')

    (4) commands, warnings, requests

    (5) exclamations, greetings.

(c) Some alternative attitudes likely to be implied by the various intonation patterns are given brief verbal descriptions in each case, but it must be remembered that the precise attitudinal connotation of intonation patterns will always depend upon the contextual situation in which they occur; further cues to attitude will also be provided by the voice quality, the pitch range and the rate of delivery with which they are said.

(d) The elements of the intonation patterns illustrated are:

    (1) all types of nucleus

(2) generally high level of syllables before the nucleus (shown as e.g. ‾‾ ◡)

(3) generally low level of syllables before the nucleus (shown as e.g. ___ ◡)

(4) falls before the nucleus (shown as e.g. ` `)

(For rises before the nucleus, see section 5.22 of this course.)

All the possible combinations of (2), (3) and (4) do not in fact occur; only the more common patterns are exemplified.

5.15 Statements

I 28 *Listen and repeat*
(◡): calmly definite; routine
ˏNo.   ˏThis is ˏmine.   ˏJohn ˏgave it to me.

I 29 *Listen and repeat*
(___ ◡): routine; lack of interest; surly
ˏThis is ˏmine.
You can ˏcome on ˏTuesday
I'd ˏlike some ˏtea.

I 30 *Listen and repeat*
(‾‾ ◡): lively; enthusiastic; forceful
'This is ˏmine.
You can 'come on ˏTuesday.
I'd 'like some ˏtea.

I 31 *Listen and repeat*
(`): strongly assertive; excited
`No!   `This is ˏmine.   `John ˏgave it to me.

I 32 *Listen and repeat*
(___ `): strongly contrastive; protesting
ˏThis is `mine!
You can ˏcome on `Tuesday!
I'd ˏlike some `tea!

I 33 *Listen and repeat*
(` `): insistence on more than one word
`This is `mine!
You can `come on `Tuesday!
I'd `like some `tea!

I 34 *Listen and repeat*
(‚): tentative; appealing; guarded; continuative
‚No. ‚John ‚liked it. ‚Some of us ‚do.

I 35 *Listen and repeat*
(___ ‚): reserved; unenthusiastic; grudging
‚This is ‚mine.
You can ‚come on ‚Tuesday.
I'd ‚like some ‚tea.
It's ‚all ‚right.

I 36 *Listen and repeat*
(___ ‚): reassuring; lively; polite; unfinished
'This is ‚mine.
You can 'come on ‚Tuesday.
I'd 'like some ‚tea.
It's 'all ‚right.

I 37 *Listen and repeat*
(pattern as in **I36**): non-final clauses)
'When we ‚got there, (they'd gone).
'If you ‚want some, (you can buy them).
I 'didn't ‚come, (because I was ill).

I 38 *Listen and repeat*
(ᵛ): strongly assertive + encouraging, pleading, doubting
ᵛNo ᵛYesterday ᵛHere it ‚is.

I 39 *Listen and repeat*
(___ ᵛ): strongly contrastive + encouraging, reproachful;
implying an alternative
You can ‚come on ᵛTuesday (but not on Monday).
I'd ‚like some ᵛtea (but not coffee).
‚John ‚gave me a ᵛbook (but not a pen).

I 40 *Listen and repeat*
(ˋ ᵛ): strongly assertive + encouraging, lively, reproachful;
also implying an alternative
You can ˋcome on ᵛTuesday.
I'd ˋlike some ᵛtea.
‚John ˋgave me a ᵛbook.

I 41 *Listen and repeat*
(ˇ): in non-final clauses—contrastive + continuative
And ˇthen, (we saw him).
On ˇMonday, (we'll be home).

I 42 *Listen and repeat*
(___ ˇ): as in **I41**
ˌWhen it had ˌstopped ˇraining, (we went out).
If ˌeveryone ˇlikes it, (we'll buy it).

I 43 *Listen and repeat*
(ˋ ˇ): non-final clauses; more lively and interested than the preceding case
ˋWhen it had ˌstopped ˇraining, (we went out).
If ˋeveryone ˇlikes it, (we'll buy it).

I 44 *Listen and repeat*
(ˋ ˌ): lively and contrastive on the fall + continuative, with an implied alternative, on the rise
ˋYou can ˌcome on ˌTuesday, (but not John).
I'd ˋlike some ˌtea, (if you don't mind).

I 45 *Listen and repeat*
(similarly with non-final clauses; more lively and contrastive than ‾‾‾ ˌ)
If you'd ˋlike some ˌtea, (I'll make some).
When ˋJohn and ˋMary ˌcome, (we'll all be here).

I 46 *Listen and repeat*
Note the additional implication associated with (ˇ) as opposed to (ˌ) or (ˋ).
I ˋliked the ˋwine. (=especially)
I ˋliked the ˇwine. (=but not the coffee)
I 'can't 'eat ˌanything. (=I can eat nothing)
I ˋcan't ˌeat ˇanything. (=I can eat *some* things)

5.16 WH questions

I 47 *Listen and repeat*
(ˌ): curt; detached; routine
ˌWhere? ˌHow? ˌWhen did you ˌcome?

I 48   *Listen and repeat*
(____ ͵): without great interest
͵What's the ͵time?
͵Who are ͵you?
͵When are you ͵coming?

I 49   *Listen and repeat*
(‾‾‾ ͵): lively; interested
'What's the ͵time?
'Who are ͵you?
'When are you ͵coming?

I 50   *Listen and repeat*
(`): excited; indignant; puzzled
`Where?    `How?   `When did you ͵come?

I 51   *Listen and repeat*
(____ `): urgent; strong emphasis
͵What's the `time?
͵Who are `you?
͵When are you `coming?

I 52   *Listen and repeat*
(‾‾‾ `): lively; very interested; affable
'What's the `time?
'Who are `you?
'When are you `coming?

I 53   *Listen and repeat*
(` `): insistent
`What's the `time?
`Who are `you?
`When are you `coming?

I 54   *Listen and repeat*
(͵): encouraging; wondering: guarded
͵Where?   ͵How?   ͵When did you ͵come?

I 55   *Listen and repeat*
(____ ͵): routine, but polite
͵What's the ͵time?
͵Who are ͵you?
͵When are you ͵coming?

I 56 *Listen and repeat*
(⎯ ͵): interested; appealing: polite
'What's the ͵time?
'Who are ͵you?
'When are you ͵coming?

I 57 *Listen and repeat*
('): seeking repetition; surprised
'Where? 'How? 'When did you ͵come?
(⎯ ') 'What's the 'time? (= Is that what you asked me?)

I 58 *Listen and repeat*
(ᵛ): forceful; encouraging; prompting
ᵛWhere? ᵛHow?
(___ ᵛ) ͵Who are ᵛyou?

I 59 *Listen and repeat*
(ˋ ͵): insistence on the fall; appealing question on the rise
ˋWhat did you ͵say?
ˋWhen are you ͵coming?
ˋWho's the ͵girl in the ͵black ͵dress?

5.17 Yes/No questions

I 60 *Listen and repeat*
(͵): curt; impatient; without interest
͵Are you ͵coming?
͵Does he ͵want to?

I 61 *Listen and repeat*
(___ ͵): perfunctory; disgruntled
͵Are you ͵coming?
͵Does he ͵want to?
͵Have you ͵got the ͵tickets?

I 62 *Listen and repeat*
(⎯ ͵): impatient; serious; hostile
'Are you ͵coming?
'Does he ͵want to?
'Have you 'got the ͵tickets?

I 63 *Listen and repeat*
(ˋ): insistent; demands an answer

(I 63) ꞌAre you ˌcoming?
ꞌDoes he ˌwant to?

I 64 *Listen and repeat*
(___ Ꞌ): as for preceding pattern
ˌAre you ꞋComing?
ˌDoes he Ꞌwant to?
ˌHave you ˌgot the Ꞌtickets?

I 65 *Listen and repeat*
(Ꞌ Ꞌ): assertive; hectoring; very emphatic
ꞋAre you ꞋComing?
ꞋDoes he Ꞌwant to?
ꞋHave you Ꞌgot the Ꞌtickets?

I 66 *Listen and repeat*
(ˌ): doubtful; gentle
ˌAre you ˌcoming?
ˌDid he ˌlike it?

I 67 *Listen and repeat*
(___ ˌ): indifferent; sceptical
ˌCan you ˌcome?
ˌDid he ˌlike it?

I 68 *Listen and repeat*
(‾‾‾ ˌ): interested; lively; polite
'Can you ˌcome?
'Does he ˌwant to?
'Did he ˌlike it?
'Have you 'got the ˌtickets?

I 69 *Listen and repeat*
(ꞌ) or (___ ꞌ): questions with this intonation are elliptical
or have the form of a statement, and seek repetition:
ꞋNow?   ToꞋmorrow?
He's ˌcoming on ꞋMonday?
or may express surprise, concern or suspicion:
ˌWill you ꞋCome? (*concern*)
It ꞋIs? (*surprised*)
ˌCan we aꞋfford it? (*anxiety*)

I 70 *Listen and repeat*

(ˇ) or (＿＿ ˇ): may have the form of a statement, and expresses astonishment:

ˇNow? Toˇday? You ˇdid?
You ˌreally ˇcan?

I 71 *Listen and repeat*

(ˋ ˌ): shows insistence on a word before the rising nucleus or may mark two clauses in a question:

ˋCan you ˌcome?
ˋHave you ˌgot the ˌtickets?
ˋWould you ˌlike some ˌtea?
ˌDid you ˋtell him you'd ˌseen me?

5.18 Question-tags

Note: These belong to the category of Yes/No questions, but particular attention should be paid to the use of a rise or a fall. When the speaker uses a rise, he seeks *information;* when he uses a fall, he seeks *confirmation* of his opinion.

I 72 *Listen and repeat* (comparison: rise and fall)

She's ˋnice, ˋisn't she?
She's ˋnice, ˌisn't she?
He ˋdoesn't, ˋdoes he?
He ˋdoesn't, ˌdoes he?
It ˌisn't ˋthere, ˌis it?
It ˌisn't ˋthere, ˋis it?

5.19 Commands, warnings, requests

Note: Since falls are typically assertive and final, they are associated with commands; rises, being typically appealing and non-final, are often used for requests; warnings may have a falling pattern if forceful, a rising pattern if gentle.

I 73 *Listen and repeat*

(ˌ): calm, quiet command
ˌWait! ˌTake it! ˌCount them!

I 74 *Listen and repeat*
(____ ⌡): perfunctory, icy command
ˌPut it ˌover ˏthere!
ˌCome ˌback ˏhere!

I 75 *Listen and repeat*
(⎺⎺⎺ ⌡): lively, strong but affable command
'Put it 'over ˏthere!
'Come 'back ˏhere!

I 76 *Listen and repeat*
(ˋ): urgent, energetic command
ˋWait! ˋDrop it! ˋListen to me!

I 77 *Listen and repeat*
(____ ˋ): strong insistence on the nucleus; energetic command
ˌGo and ˋfind it!
ˌPut it ˌover ˋthere!

I 78 *Listen and repeat*
(⎺⎺⎺ ⌡): the same attitude as for the previous pattern, but the high syllables before the nucleus lessen the insistence on the nucleus; often impatient
'Go and ˏfind it!
'Put it 'over ˏthere!

I 79 *Listen and repeat*
(ˋ ˋ): the same attitude as for the previous pattern, but with greater insistence on words before the nucleus; may show great irritation
ˋGo and ˋfind it!
ˋPut it ˋover ˋthere!

I 80 *Listen and repeat*
(ˏ): the rising pattern being gentler and more encouraging, it is typical of mild commands, warnings and requests
ˏWait! ˏListen! ˏGive it to me!

I 81 *Listen and repeat*
(____ ˏ): routine request or command
ˌSit ˏdown! ˌCome ˌover ˏhere! ˌShut the ˏdoor!

I 82 *Listen and repeat*
(‾‾‾‚): polite, lively request
'Sit ‚down!   'Come 'over ‚here!   'Shut the ‚door!

I 83 *Listen and repeat*
(ᵛ): lively, encouraging; soothing; reproachful; but urgent command
ᵛWait!   ᵛListen!   ᵛTry it!

I 84 *Listen and repeat*
(___ ᵛ): as for the previous pattern
‚Hold it ᵛgently!
‚Don't ‚make a ᵛnoise!

I 85 *Listen and repeat*
(ˋ ᵛ): as for the previous pattern, but with insistence on words before the nucleus
ˋHold it ᵛgently!
ˋDon't ‚make a ᵛnoise!

I 86 *Listen and repeat*
(ˋ ‚): sympathetic; encouraging; pleading
ˋTake ‚care!
ˋDon't ‚make a ‚noise!
ˋDo ‚sit ‚down!
ˋShut the ‚door!
ˋMind ‚how you ‚go!

5.20 Exclamations and greetings

I 87 *Listen and repeat*
(‚): perfunctory greeting or casual exclamation
‚Morning!   ‚Really!   ‚Dreadful!
on a very low pitch, may express incredulity or horror
‚No!   ‚Idiot!

I 88 *Listen and repeat*
(___ ‚): perfunctory; bored; unconcerned
‚Good ‚morning.   ‚How a‚nnoying!   ‚What a ‚mess!

I 89 *Listen and repeat*
(‾‾‾ ‚): more lively and interested
'Good ‚morning!   'Fancy ‚that!   'What a ‚mess!

I 90   *Listen and repeat*
('): hearty; enthusiastic; surprised
'Morning!   'Really!   'What a sur,prise!

I 91   *Listen and repeat*
(___ '): bright; enthusiastic; surprised
,Good 'morning!   Hu'llo!   ,How 'nice!   ,Fancy 'that!

I 92   *Listen and repeat*
(' '): very strong, with reinforcement of words or syllables
before the nucleus
,Good 'after'noon!
'What an 'awful 'film that was!
'How on 'earth can you 'eat it!

I 93   *Listen and repeat*
(,): perfunctory; reserved; cautious
,Morning!   ,Really!

I 94   *Listen and repeat*
(___ ,): friendly, but casual or cautious
,Good ,morning!   Hu,llo!   ,Good ,luck!

I 95   *Listen and repeat*
(⎯ ,): cheerful; lively
'Good ,morning!   'Hu,llo!   'Good ,luck!

I 96   *Listen and repeat*
(ⱽ) or (___ ⱽ): incredulity; scorn
ⱽReally!   Aⱽgain!   He ,says he ⱽdoes!

I 97   *Listen and repeat*
(' ,): warm; friendly; encouraging
'Good ,morning!   'Well ,done!   'Bad ,luck!

5.21   Rise-fall nucleus (^)

Note: A rise-fall nucleus may be used instead of a high-fall for
extra insistence or emphasis; in any case, it often happens that the
high-fall is preceded by a slight rise.

I 98   *Listen and repeat*
^No!   ,This is ^mine!
,Who are ^you?   ,Can you be ^sure?

ˌBe ˌthere on ^time!
ˌGood ^morning!   ^Really!

5.22   Rises before the nucleus

Note: Rises before the nucleus may often express an irritable, impatient or complaining attitude.

I 99   *Listen and repeat*
ˌThese were the ˌonly ˌgrapes I could ˋfind.
ˌWho do you ˌthink you ˋare?
ˌHaven't you ˌfound the ˌtickets ˌyet?
ˌWhat a ˌmess you've ˌmade in the ˋgarden!

5.23   Dialogue 1

I 100   *Listen* to the dialogue until you can understand it without difficulty; then, look at the phonetic transcription in Appendix p. 78, noting the implication of the intonation patterns. The style is normal, familiar colloquial.

George: Mary! I'll be off now then, What time did you say we'd go to the Robinsons?

Mary: Well, I told them seven; but I thought you'd be at home for the day when I said that. I'll make it later if you like.

George: Oh, it doesn't matter. I can get away by five, I should think. Is anyone else I know going?

Mary: Only John Murray. You've met him before.

George: Who? Murray? Oh yes, he was at that party that Susan gave, wasn't he?

Mary: That's right. It was only last Friday, you know. You ought to remember him.

George: Oh, I remember the man, now you mention it. It's names I forget nowadays. Must be getting old!

Mary: Yes, you are! But don't worry! You're not as old as you look. Just don't forget to be home before seven though.

George: I won't. But I'll have to go now, or I'll miss my train. Goodbye!

I 101 *Listen and repeat* the dialogue, which is now said with pauses

5.24 **Dialogue 2.** (not recorded)
Transcribe the following dialogue and compare your version with that given in Appendix p. 80.

George: Here I am, Mary! I told you I wouldn't be late.

Mary: Well done! I was afraid something might happen to keep you at the office. Still, you'd better get a move on, even so.

George: I say! You *are* looking glamorous! Have I seen that dress before?

Mary: Of course you have. I've had it for years. Aren't you going to change? That's a very shiny old suit you've got on.

George: I suppose I ought to with you looking so smart. Pity! I feel comfortable in this—it's sort of lived in. Still, I'll put the blue one on—even if it is a bit tight round the middle. Just give me five minutes.

Mary: No more! It's usually only a quarter of an hour to the Robinsons by car, but the traffic can be awful at this time of the evening. So we'd better leave a bit sooner, just in case. I'll get the car out, if you'll give me the keys.

George: Car keys? Funny! I don't seem to have them. I must have left them in the car. Silly of me!

Appendix

In the following pages, answers are given for the *Identification* and *Transcription* drills in Sections 2–5.

V2   (1) uː   (2) ɑː   (3) ɔː   (4) ɜː   (5) iː
    (6) ɑː   (7) iː   (8) uː   (9) ɜː   (10) ɔː
    (11) uː   (12) ɜː   (13) ɔː   (14) iː   (15) ɜː

V3   (1) uː   (2) ɜː   (3) ɔː   (4) **X**   (5) iː
    (6) **X**   (7) ɔː   (8) ɑː   (9) ɜː   (10) **X**
    (11) uː   (12) **X**   (13) iː   (14) **X**   (15) ɔː

V7   The vowels are too long in: *feet, loose, sauce*.

V11   (1) e   (2) ɒ   (3) ʊ   (4) ɪ   (5) æ
    (6) ɒ   (7) ʌ   (8) ə   (9) ʊ   (10) ə
    (11) ʌ   (12) ʊ   (13) æ   (14) e   (15) ɪ
    (16) ə   (17) ʌ   (18) e   (19) æ   (20) ɪ

V12   (1) e   (2) **X**   (3) ʊ   (4) ɒ   (5) ə
    (6) **X**   (7) æ   (8) e   (9) **X**   (10) ʌ
    (11) ɒ   (12) **X**   (13) ə   (14) ɪ   (15) ʌ

V14   (1) ɪ   (2) e   (3) ɪ   (4) ɪ   (5) e

V16   (1) æ   (2) e   (3) e   (4) æ   (5) e   (6) æ

V18   (1) ʌ   (2) ʌ   (3) æ   (4) ʌ   (5) æ   (6) æ

V20   (1) ɒ   (2) ʌ   (3) ɒ   (4) ɒ   (5) ʌ   (6) ɒ

V22   (1) ə   (2) ə   (3) ɪ   (4) ɪ   (5) ə   (6) ə

V26   (1) ɪt   (2) ɔːt   (3) ʊt   (4) ɜːt   (5) iːt
    (6) æt   (7) ɑːd   (8) iːd   (9) ʌd   (10) et
    (11) ʊd   (12) uːd   (13) ət   (14) ɑːt   (15) ɜːd

V28   (1) iː   (2) e   (3) **X** (wrong quality)   (4) ɒ
    (5) ɔː   (6) **X** (wrong quality)
    (7) **X** (wrong quality)   (8) ɜː   (9) ʌ

(10) **X** (too long)　　(11) æ
(12) **X** (wrong quality, too long)　　　　(13) ɑː
(14) **X** (wrong quality)　　(15) ɒ
(16) **X** (*r* wrongly inserted)　　(17) uː　(18) ɪ

V31　(1) eɪ　(2) ɔɪ　(3) aɪ　(4) eɪ
　　　(5) aɪ　(6) ɔɪ　(7) eɪ　(8) aɪ

V32　(1) eɪ　(2) ɔɪ　(3) aɪ
　　　(4) **X** (too close second element)　　(5) aɪ
　　　(6) **X** (too close—both elements)　　(7) eɪ
　　　(8) **X** (wrong quality—first element)

V35　The diphthongs are too long in: *wait, light.*

V39　(1) əʊ　(2) aʊ　(3) aʊ　(4) əʊ　(5) aʊ　(6) əʊ

V40　(1) əʊ　(2) aʊ　(3) əʊ　(4) **X** (wrong first element)
　　　(5) əʊ　(6) aʊ　(7) **X** (wrong first element)　(8) əʊ

V43　The diphthongs are too long in: *won't, mouth.*

V51　(1) ɛə　(2) ʊə　(3) ɪə　(4) ʊə
　　　(5) ɛə　(6) ɪə　(7) ʊə　(8) ɪə

V52　(1) ɪə　(2) ɛə　(3) ɪə　(4) ʊə
　　　(5) **X** (first element too close and tense)　　(6) ɛə
　　　(7) **X** (first element too close and tense)　　(8) ɪə

V56　(1) vəliːləʊ　(2) bendɒsə　(3) taɪpʊt
　　　(4) saːkuːt　(5) dʌnekt　(6) fɜːmɪə
　　　(7) əmɔːkɪ　(8) vəʊpɔɪ

V57　(1) gɜːlɪk　(2) sXbə　(3) kæmɒn
　　　(4) həʊvXn　(5) mʌspiːp　(6) fɔːtɪə
　　　(7) vXlən　(8) baɪfəʊs

V58　dɪsɔːgənaɪz　spiːdɒmɪtə　rɪpʌlsɪv
　　　smɔːlpɒks　səlɪləkwɪ　ləʊkəməʊtɪv
　　　esɪks　kəʊələs　pærədɒks
　　　kʌntrɪmən　benɪfæktə　wɜːkbaːskɪt

C2　/t/ in *time*;　/g/ in *game*;　/p/ in *pen*;　/b/ in *bone*;
　　　/t/ **X** (incorrectly dental) in *ten*;　/d/ in *die*;　/t/ in *tea*;
　　　/g/ in *egg*;　/d/ **X** (incorrectly dental) in *said*;　/t/ in *eat*

C5 /k/ in *come*; /t/ in *ten*; /p/ in *pin*; /t/ X (unaspirated) in *town*; /d/ in *do*; /k/ X (unaspirated) in *came*; /d/ in *dear*; /p/ X (unaspirated) in *pie*; /t/ in *toe*; /p/ in *pair*

C9 /t/ in *stone*; /k/ in *skin*; /p/ X (wrongly aspirated) in *spin*; /t/ in *steam*; /p/ in *spare*; /k/ X (wrongly aspirated) in *sky*; /t/ in *stay*; /p/ X (wrongly aspirated) in *spoon*

C14 Incorrect aspiration after /p/ in *wiped*;
intrusive vowel after /d/ in *goodbye*;
incorrect aspiration of /k/ in *sector*

C18 Intrusive vowel after /b/ in *submit*;
incorrect aspiration of /t/ in *written*;
intrusive vowel after /d/ in *madness*

C23 Incorrect aspiration after /t/ in *cattle*;
intrusive vowel after /d/ in *idle*

C26 (1) tʃɑː (2) trɑː (3) dʒɑː (4) drɑː
(5) truː (6) dʒuː (7) druː (8) tʃuː

C34 (1) sɑː (2) ɑːθə (3) ɑːʃ (4) fɑː
(5) ɑːð (6) ɑːʒə (7) hɑː (8) θɑː
(9) ɑːsə (10) ɑːðə (11) ɑːʃə (12) ɑːθ

C50 (1) ɪn (2) ɪŋ (3) ɪŋə (4) ɪn
(5) ɪnə (6) ɪŋ (7) ɪŋə

C52 (1) ɪŋ (2) ɪŋə (3) ɪŋgə (4) ɪŋə
(5) ɪŋk (6) ɪŋ (7) ɪŋkə (8) ɪŋgə

C58 (1) l (2) ɫ (3) ɫ (4) l
(5) ɫ (6) ɫ (7) l (8) ɫ

C59 incorrect 'clear' [l] in *told, healthy, table*;
incorrect 'dark' [ɫ] in *life*

C62 Incorrect full voicing of [l] in *clean, plan*

C66 (1) rɑː (2) Xɑː (3) ɑːrə (4) rɑː
(5) Xɑː (6) ɑːrə (7) ɑːXə (8) rɑː

C72 r-sounds incorrectly inserted in *farm, dear, learn*

C75 (1) lɑː   (2) ɑːrə   (3) rɑː   (4) blɑː
      (5) rɑː   (6) ɑːlə   (7) glɑː   (8) frɑː
      (9) brɑː   (10) grɑː   (11) flɑː   (12) ɑːrə

C82 (1) veɪ   (2) wɜː   (3) waɪ   (4) viː
      (5) weɪ   (6) vɜː

A2 (1) 'lɪlɪ   (2) lɪ'lɪ   (3) lɪ'lɪ
     (4) 'lɪlɪ   (5) 'lɪlɪ   (6) lɪ'lɪ

A3 ə'nəɪ;   'ɑːmə;   'səʊfə;   pə'liːs;   'mɑːbl;   bɪ'ləʊ

A11 (1) lə'lɑːlə   (2) 'lɑːlələ   (3) lɪ'lɪlə   (4) 'lɪlɪlə

A12 'kwɒlətɪ   ɪ'nɔːməs   kən'teɪnə
      sə'luːʃn   'lʌkəlɪ   'kærəktə

A15 (Remember secondary accent is marked with ˌ.)
     (1) 'lɑːlə͵lɑː   (2) ͵lɔːlɪ'luː   (3) ͵lɑː'lɔːlɪ
     (4) lə'leɪlɔː   (5) ͵mɜːnə'laʊ   (6) fə'dɑːməʊ

A19 (1) *adj.*   (2) *n.*   (3) *vb.*   (4) *n.*
     (5) *vb.*   (6) *vb.*   (7) *n.*   (8) *vb.*

A22 (1) lə'lɑːlələ   (2) ͵lɑː'lɑːlələ   (3) ͵lɑːlə'lɑːlə
     (4) 'lɑːlə͵lɑːlə   (5) 'lɑːlələ͵lɑː   (6) ͵lɑːlələ'lɑː
     (7) 'lɑːlələlə   (8) lə'lɑːlə͵lɑː   (9) ͵lɑːlə'lɑːlə
     (10) ͵lɑː'lɑːlələ

A31 ɪ'njuːmə͵reɪt   θɜː'tiːn   'kɒnstɪ͵peɪtɪd   ə'ləʊn
     ͵ɪnvɪ'teɪʃn   'pærə͵grɑːf   'ʌndə   'ɔːtəmə͵biːl
     mə'rakəʊ   'sʌb'nɔːml   'sɜːtʃlaɪt   ͵suːpərɪn'tend

A56 Accents on the following syllables:
     (1) course — want — come
     (2) chil— — like — run — —bout
     (3) That's — way — do
     (4) could — come — Tues— — night
     (5) came — time — tea

A59 Accents on the following syllables:
     (1) all — find
     (2) ev— — thought — te—
     (3) one — books — ta—
     (4) When — —rived — dark

A60 Accents on the following syllables:
(1) hun— — —le—
(2) How — proved
(3) Some — —prised
(4) See — find — kit—

A64 Accents on the following syllables:
(1) all — ve— — wel
(2) gave — ten — days — no—
(3) no — good — cry— — spilt — milk

A81 (1) ðeɪ wə ðə 'fɜːst tʊ ə'raɪv ət ðɪ 'entrəns.
(2) 'wɒt ə jʊ 'ɡəʊɪŋ tə 'brɪŋ əs frəm 'lʌndən?
(3) hiː wəz 'weɪtɪŋ ət ðə 'kɔːnə fər ən 'ɑːə.
(4) aɪ 'təʊld ðəm ðət ðə wəz ə 'lɒt əv ɪt ə'baʊt.
(5) 'dʒæks 'nɒt 'ʃɔːr ɪf iː kən 'kʌm.
(6) 'kæn aɪ 'ɡet tə ðə 'strænd baɪ 'bʌs?
(7) aɪ 'θɔːt iːd 'ɡet 'mɔ: 'vəʊts ðn iː 'dɪd.

Additional drills (not recorded)
(1) hiː kəd əv 'bɔːt sʌm əv ðəm, ɪf iːd 'hæd ə 'bɑːskɪt.
(2) əz 'fɑːr əz aɪ 'nəʊ, wɪ 'wəʊnt bɪ 'ðɛə tɪl 'ten.
(3) 'wɒt ʃl wɪ 'duː ɪf 'dʒɒnz 'leɪt?
(4) ə'baʊt 'wen dəz iː ɪk'spekt tʊ ə'raɪv?
(5) aɪ 'θɔːt ðə wə səm 'mɑːvələs 'pleɪəz ˌðɛə.

I 2 *Nucleus (initiation of pitch change) on:*
(1) my   (2) book   (3) This   (4) is   (5) com—
(6) you   (7) Are   (8) want   (9) tea   (10) don't

I 5 *Changes of pitch direction on:*
(1) This — my   (2) How — stamps — John
(3) Su— — there   (4) Do — want
(5) That — nice

I 8 (1) ˈNo   (2) ˌNo   (3) ˌNo   (4) ˈNo   (5) ˇNo
(6) ˌNo   (7) ˈNo   (8) ˈNo   (9) ˌNo   (10) ˇNo

I 11 (1) ˈmine   (2) ˇtwo   (3) ˌlate   (4) aˈlone
(5) baˇlloon   (6) ˌnot   (7) perˌhaps   (8) surˈprised

I 15 (1) Toˈmorrow   (2) It's ˈSaturday   (3) We exˇpected it.
(4) She ˌtold him to   (5) He ˌwanted to.

I 20   *Pitch level of accented syllables before the nucleus generally:*
(1) high   (2) low   (3) low   (4) high   (5) high   (6) low

I 27   'Where's the ˌteleˌphone diˌrectory?
I 'want 'John's ˎphone ˌnumber.
ˌHow is it he ˌspells his ˌsurname?
There's an ˎ'e' at the ˌend of ˌBrowne, ˌisn't there?
ˎHere it ˌis. '3'4ˌ8 '6'2'8ˌ7
Is 'that ˌyou, ˌJohn?
Oh, ˎMrs ˌBrowne.
I 'quite 'thought it was ˎJohn.
'Is he 'likely to be ˌhome ˌsoon?
I 'wanted to 'have a ˎword with him aˌbout my 'new ˌtape-
reˌcorder.
It's ˎprobably ˎmy ˌfault, but I 'can't 'seem to 'get it to ˌwork.

Dialogue 1   I 100–101

George: ˎmɛərɪ!
calling, friendly with fall-rise

ɑɪl bɪ ˎɒf ˌnɑʊ ðen.
fall+rise, inviting response

ˌwɒt ˌtaɪm dʒʊ ˌseɪ wiːd ˌgəʊ tə ðə ˌrɒbɪnsnz?
*insistence on re-statement of time with nucleus on 'what';
note compression of 'did you'*

Mary: wel aɪ ˎtəʊld ðəm ˎsevn,
*'well' is a 'filler' without accent; strong accents on 'told'
and 'seven'*

bət aɪ 'θɔːtʃuːd bɪ ət ˎhəʊm fə ðə ˌdeɪ,
*nuclear insistence on 'home'; assimilation /t+j/ to /tʃ/ in
'thought you'*

wen aɪ ˌsed ˌðæt.
rise for dependent clause

aɪl ˌmeɪk ɪt ˎleɪtər ɪf jʊ ˌlaɪk.
*insistence on 'later', rise on 'like' as dependent clause;
linking /r/ in 'later if'*

George: əʊ ɪt ˌdʌznt ˌmætə
'oh' is a 'filler'—no accent; low pitch before low rising nucleus shows slight annoyance

aɪ kŋ ˌget əˌweɪ baɪ ˌfaɪv aɪ ʃd ˌθɪŋk.
continues with disgruntled attitude with low rise on 'five' and pre-nuclear low pitch; 'can' assimilates to /kŋ/ before 'get'; 'should' reduced to /ʃd/

ɪz ˈenɪwʌn ˌels aɪ ˌnəʊ ˌgəʊɪŋ?
nucleus on 'else'; high pre-nuclear syllables show interest

Mary: ˋəʊnlɪ ˌdʒɒn ˌmʌrɪ.
fall + rise, reassuring

juːv ˋmet ˌhɪm brˋfɔː
insistent falls on 'met, before'; stressed 'him' keeps /h/

George: ˊhuː? ˊmʌrɪ?
high rises seeking clarification

əʊ ˌjes. ˌhiː wəz̄ət ˌðæt ˌpɑːtɪ ðət ˋsuːzn ˌgeɪv, ˌwɔznt iː?
secondary accent on 'he'; focus of prominence on 'Susan'; rise on question-tag seeks information

Mary: ˋðæts ˌraɪt.
fall + rise, friendly agreement

ɪt wəz ˋəʊnlɪ ˌlɑːst ˋfraɪdɪ ju ˌnəʊ.
falls + rise, reproachful attitude

ju ˋɔːt tə rɪˌmembər ɪm.
fall + rise, reproachful; linking /r/ and loss of /h/ in 'remember him'

George: əʊ ˋaɪ rɪˌmembə ðə ˌmæn, ˌnaʊ ju ˌmenʃn ɪt.
fall + rise show two points of information focus; low-rise nucleus in dependent clause

ɪts ˋneɪmz aɪ fəˌget ˌnɑːdeɪz.
fall + rise, excusing; /aʊə/ in 'nowadays' reduced to /ɑːə/

ˌmʌs bɪ ˌgetɪŋ ˋəʊld.
elision of 'I' and /t/ of 'must'; nuclear focus on 'old'

Mary: ˋjes ju ˋɑː! bət ˋdəʊnt ˌwʌrɪ!
two high-falls, strong agreement; comforting fall + rise on 'don't worry'

juə ˋnɒt əz ˌəʊld əʒuː ˌlʊk.
fall + rise, humouring; /z + j/ in 'as you' assimilates to /ʒ/

ˈdʒʌs ˈdaʊnt fəˈget tə bɪ ˈhəʊm brɪˈfɔː ˌsevn ˌðəʊ.
low-fall nucleus, matter-of-fact; elision of /t/ in 'just'

George: ˋaɪ ˌwəʊnt.
fall + rise, reassuring

bət aɪl ˈhæf tə ˋgəʊ ˌnɑʊ.
fall + rise, urgent with implication; /v/ of 'have' assimilates to /f/ before /t/

ɔːr aɪl ˋmɪs maɪ ˋtreɪn.
two high-falls focus attention on 'miss, train'

ˈgʊbˌbaɪ!
high pre-nuclear 'good', cheerful; low-rise, friendly; /d/ of 'good' assimilates to /b/ before 'bye'

Dialogue 2

George: ˋhɪər aɪ ˌæm, ˌmɛərɪ! aɪ ˋtəʊldʒʊ aɪ ˌwʊdn bɪ ˌleɪt.

Mary: ˋwel ˋdʌn! aɪ wəz əˌfreɪd ˌsʌmθɪŋ ˌmaɪt ˌhæpn tə ˌkiːp jʊ ət ðɪ ˋɒfɪs. ˈstɪl, jʊəd ˋbetə ˌget ə ˈmuːv ˌɒn, ˌiːvn ˋsəʊ.

George: ˋaɪ ˋseɪ, ˋjuː ˋɑː ˌlʊkɪŋ ˌglæmərəs! həv ˈaɪ ˈsiːn ˈðæt ˈdres bɪˌfɔː?

Mary: f ˋkɔːs jʊ ˌhæv. aɪv ˌhæd ɪt fə ˋjɜːz. ˈɑːntʃʊ ˈgəʊɪŋ tə ˌtʃeɪndʒ? ˋðæts ə ˋverɪ ˋʃaɪnɪ ˌəʊld ˋsuːt juːv ˌgɒt ˌɒn.

George: aɪ ˌspəʊz aɪ ˋɔːt tuː, wɪð ˌjuː ˌlʊkɪŋ səʊ ˌsmɑːt. ˇpɪtɪ! aɪ ˌfiːl ˋkʌmftəbl ɪn ˌðis—ɪts ˌsɔːt əv ˋlɪvd ɪn. ˈstɪl, aɪl ˈpʊt ðə ˋbluː wʌn ɒn, iːvn ɪf ɪt ˋɪz ə ˌbit ˌtaɪt ˌraʊnd ðə ˌmɪdl. ˈdʒʌs ˈgɪv mɪ ˈfaɪv ˌmɪnɪts.

Mary: ˋnəʊ ˇmɔː! ɪts ˋjuːʒəlɪ ˌəʊnlɪ ə ˋkwɔːtrəv n ˋɑːə tə ðə rɒbɪnsnz baɪ ˌkɑː, bət ðə ˋtræfɪk kəm bɪ ˋɔːfl ət ˌðis ˌtaɪm əv ðɪ ˌiːvnɪŋ. sə wiːd ˈbetə ˈliːv ə bɪt ˋsuːnə, ˋdʒʌst ɪŋ ˋkeɪs. aɪl ˈget ðə ˋkɑːr ˌaʊt, ɪf juːl ˌgɪv mɪ ðə ˌkiːz.

George: ˌkɑː ˈkiːz? ˌfʌnɪ! aɪ ˌdəʊnt ˌsiːm tə ˋhæv ðəm. aɪ ˌmʌst əv ˌleft ðəm ɪn ðə ˋkɑː. ˋsɪlɪ ɒv mɪ!